LEVEL THREE

Sound Advice
Theory and Ear Training

Brenda Braaten and **Crystal Wiksyk**

Series Editor
Laura Beauchamp-Williamson

Illustrations by Paul McCusker

© Copyright 2006 The Frederick Harris Music Co., Limited
All Rights Reserved

ISBN 1-55440-033-3

Sound Advice Audio Tracks—Online

Your purchase of this book includes access to all of the audio tracks you need to complete the Ear-Training Worksheets for *Sound Advice* Level 3. Visit www.soundadvicedirect.com and log on using this password:

yktxabg6

The *Sound Advice* website allows you to download the recordings according to your needs: one level at a time, one lesson at a time, or one track at a time. Depending on the resources available to you, you can listen to the tracks on your computer, copy the tracks to a CD, or import the tracks to your digital music player.

On the *Sound Advice* website, you will find step-by-step instructions for downloading the tracks, helpful FAQs, and contact information.

Reproduction of any part of this book without permission of the publisher is not permitted.

Library and Archives Canada Cataloguing in Publication

Braaten, Brenda, 1952-
Sound advice : theory and ear training / Brenda Braaten and Crystal Wiksyk ; illustrations by Paul McCusker.

Accompanied by audio tracks, available online.
To be complete in 8 vol.
Complete contents: Level 1 – Level 2 – Level 3 – Level 4 – Level 5 -- Level 6 – Level 7 – Level 8.
ISBN 1-55440-031-7 (v. 1).–ISBN 1-55440-032-5 (v. 2).–
ISBN 1-55440-033-3 (v. 3).–ISBN 1-55440-034-1 (v. 4).–
ISBN 1-55440-035-X (v. 5).–ISBN 1-55440-036-8 (v. 6).–
ISBN 1-55440-037-6 (v. 7).–ISBN 1-55440-038-4 (v. 8)

1. Music theory. 2. Ear training. I. Wiksyk, Crystal, 1959-
II. McCusker, Paul   III. Title.

MT7.B794S72 2006   781   C2005-907128-1

Contents

Preface for Teachers 6

How to Use This Book 7
Lesson Organization
Completing the Ear-Training Worksheets
Charts and Games
Suggestions for Daily Ear-Training Practice

Lesson 1

Learning Guide 10
Review of Note Values and Rests
Note-Value Comparison Chart
Ties and Dots
Rhythmic Reading
Rhythm Jumble
Theory Worksheet 13
Ear-Training Worksheet 15

Lesson 2

Learning Guide 16
Half Steps and Whole Steps
Accidentals
Enharmonic Equivalents
Theory Worksheet 18
Ear-Training Worksheet 20

Lesson 3

Learning Guide 21
Beaming Notes to Show the Beat
Circling the Beat
Rhythmic Dictation
Theory Worksheet 23
Ear-Training Worksheet 24

Lesson 4

Learning Guide 25
Meter and Time Signatures
Theory Worksheet 26
Ear-Training Worksheet 28

Lesson 5

Learning Guide 29
Major Scale Review: C, G, D, and F Major
Scale Degree Numbers
The B♭ Major Scale
Sight Singing
Theory Worksheet 31
Ear-Training Worksheet 32

Lesson 6

Learning Guide 33
Key Signatures
Theory Worksheet 34
Ear-Training Worksheet 35

Lesson 7

Learning Guide 36
Naming Intervals
Naming Minor Intervals
The Sound of the Major 2nd, Major 3rd, and Perfect 5th
Theory Worksheet 38
Ear-Training Worksheet 40

Lesson 8

Learning Guide 41
Incomplete Measures
Scale Degree Names
The Sound of the Perfect 4th
Theory Worksheet 43
Ear-Training Worksheet 44

Lesson 9

Learning Guide 45
Major and Minor 2nds: A Shortcut
Mad Music Game: Name the 2nds
The Sound of the Minor 2nd
Theory Worksheet 47
Ear-Training Worksheet 48

Lesson 10

Learning Guide 49
  A Closer Look at Writing Scales
  Writing Scales with Key Signatures
  Writing Scales with Accidentals
  Chromatic Notes
Theory Worksheet 51
Ear-Training Worksheet 52

Lesson 11

Learning Guide 53
  Major and Minor 3rds: A Shortcut
  The Sound of the Minor 3rd
  Measure Numbers
Theory Worksheet 55
Ear-Training Worksheet 56

Lesson 12

Learning Guide 57
  Major Triads
  A Stack of 3rds
  A Closer Look at the Minor 3rd
  Rhythm Jumble Games
Theory Worksheet 59
Ear-Training Worksheet 60

Lesson 13

Learning Guide 61
  Phrases
  Cadences
  Melodic Imitation
  Composing and Improvising
  The Sound of the Descending Major 2nd
  The Sound of the Descending Perfect 4th
Theory Worksheet 63
Ear-Training Worksheet 64

Lesson 14

Learning Guide 65
  Minor Triads
  The Sound of the Descending Perfect 5th
Theory Worksheet 67
Ear-Training Worksheet 68

Lesson 15

Learning Guide 69
  A Closer Look at Rests
  New Rhythmic Unit ♪
  A Closer Look at Note Values
Theory Worksheet 71
Ear-Training Worksheet 72

Lesson 16

Learning Guide 74
  Arpeggios
  The Sound of the Perfect Octave
  New Rhythmic Unit ♫
  Stem Direction
Theory Worksheet 76
Ear-Training Worksheet 77

Lesson 17

Learning Guide 79
  Rhythmic Imitation
Theory Worksheet 80
Ear-Training Worksheet 81

Lesson 18

Learning Guide 82
  Melodic Imitation
  The Sound of the Major 6th
  Song Clues for the Major 6th
Theory Worksheet 84
Ear-Training Worksheet 85

Lesson 19

Learning Guide 86
  Texture in Music
  Polyphonic Texture
  Homophonic Texture
  The Whole Rest
Theory Worksheet 88
Ear-Training Worksheet 89

Lesson 20

Learning Guide 90
Consonance and Dissonance
The Sound of the Major 7th
Musical Style
Theory Worksheet 91
Ear-Training Worksheet 92

Lesson 21

Learning Guide 93
Expression Markings
Dynamic Markings
Theory Worksheet 94
Ear-Training Worksheet 96

Lesson 22

Learning Guide 97
Review of Baroque Style
Musical Style of the Classical Period
Keyboard Instruments in the Classical Period
Theory Worksheet 99
Ear-Training Worksheet 100

Lesson 23

Learning Guide 101
The Orchestra
The Baroque Orchestra
The Classical Orchestra
Theory Worksheet 102
Ear-Training Worksheet 103

Lesson 24

Learning Guide 104
Composers of the Classical Period
Theory Worksheet 105
Ear-Training Worksheet 106

Theory Examination 107

Melody Master 110

Charts and Games

Drawing Symbols Chart 114
Rhythm Jumble Chart 115
Rhythm Jumble Games 116
Terms and Symbols Chart 117
Song Clue Chart 119
Mad Music Game 120

Answer Keys

Ear-Training 122
Melody Master 146
Mad Music Chart Answer Key 149

Appendix

Sight-Singing Syllable Systems 150

Preface for Teachers

Too often, music theory instruction emphasizes written concepts, with little or no attention paid to the way things actually *sound*. Our teaching philosophy is simple: never take the *sound* out of music theory instruction!

The *Sound Advice* program relates musical sounds to their symbols by combining written and aural theory. Throughout the series, theoretical concepts are introduced in a clear, concise manner and immediately reinforced with written worksheets and ear-training assignments. Students are also provided with lessons on musical style and an introduction to improvisation and composition.

Students of all instruments, including those who study voice, can use *Sound Advice*. Ideally, the program should be started under the guidance of a teacher as early as possible in a student's musical training. *Sound Advice* can be used successfully in private lessons, small group sessions, or in classroom teaching. On average, most private students will complete one lesson per week, while students in semester-long theory or musicianship classes may progress at a faster pace. Either way, the lesson planning is taken care of for teachers. Each lesson is carefully organized so that students are presented with an appropriate amount of new material while continuing to review previously introduced concepts. Constant review is an important feature of *Sound Advice*.

Each *Sound Advice* lesson consists of a Learning Guide that introduces new material, a written Theory Worksheet, and an Ear-Training Worksheet to be completed using the accompanying recordings. There are also a number of Charts and Games that reinforce material learned in the lessons.

Ear-training activities in Level 3 include sight singing of melodies and rhythms, rhythm singbacks and clapbacks, melody playbacks and singbacks, editing (error detection), rhythmic and melodic dictation, improvisation, and identification of intervals, triads, meter, and texture. Answers to all of the ear-training activities in *Sound Advice* can be checked by the student. We have provided Ear-Training Answer Keys so that students can mark their work at home immediately after completing each exercise. Teachers can easily monitor their students' ear-training progress by viewing the marked pages at the next lesson. Ear-training exercises can be repeated as many times as necessary for extra practice. Written Theory Worksheets are to be marked by the teacher.

It is important that teachers and students, as well as parents, understand the *How to Use This Book* section (pp. 7–9). For younger students, the teacher's guidance may be needed to get them started.

While *Sound Advice* can be used to prepare students for the ear-training and theory components of several major examining boards,[1] our main goal is to help *all* students become musically literate—to have a better understanding of how music "works" and to continue to develop a deeper appreciation for music throughout their lives.

Brenda Braaten and *Crystal Wiksyk*

---

[1] Level 3 covers ear-training requirements for The Royal Conservatory of Music (RCM) Grade 3 piano and voice examinations, Victoria Conservatory of Music (VCM) Grade 3 theory and musicianship examinations, and most Level 3 requirements of other examining boards and music teachers' associations. We strongly recommend that teachers consult current syllabi of specific examining boards for their requirements in each grade.

How to Use This Book

Lesson Organization

Each *Sound Advice* lesson contains three parts:

Learning Guide
The Learning Guides explain and visually illustrate new concepts. When beginning each lesson, you should always study the learning guide before completing the Theory Worksheet and the Ear-Training Worksheet.

Theory Worksheet
The Theory Worksheets contain written exercises for both new and review concepts. Your teacher will mark them for you when they are completed.

Ear-Training Worksheet
The Ear-Training Worksheets involve singing melodies and rhythms, performing melody playbacks/singbacks and rhythm clapbacks/singbacks, completing dictation and improvisation activities, and identifying intervals, triads, arpeggios, homophonic and polyphonic textures, and duple and triple meters. Detailed instructions are provided below. You can check you answers to these assignments yourself, using the Ear-Training Answer Key at the back of the book.

Completing the Ear-Training Worksheets

You will need to go online to access the audio tracks for *Sound Advice* Level 3 to complete the Ear-Training Worksheets. In this book, the track numbers for each exercise are identified by an icon in the margin. The instructions for each exercise will be read aloud on the recording for the first three lessons only. Beginning with Lesson 4, you must read the instructions for each question yourself. Take time to read the instructions *before* you listen to the recorded examples.

For sight-singing and rhythmic-reading questions, you should pause the recording and perform each example by yourself first, tapping a steady quarter-note beat with your finger while you sing. To check your accuracy, sing the example a second time while listening to the recording and following along in the answer key.

When you are asked to sing in an example that is out of your vocal range, you can sing it in a different octave, or internalize the sound (sing it in your head).

Sight-singing melodies and rhythms will be played once on the recording. All the other ear-training examples will be played twice, but you may replay them as many times as necessary. On the Ear-Training Worksheets, you will be asked to record the number of times you listened. Your eventual goal is to complete each question after hearing the recorded example just twice.

When you finish an activity, turn immediately to the Ear-Training Answer Key to mark your work. *Do not erase your mistakes and replace them with the correct answers.* Instead, write in the correct answers *above* the errors. If you correct your work this way, you and your teacher will be able to look back at your progress over several lessons and identify areas that need extra practice.

Important: If you make a mistake on an ear-training question, always go back and listen to the recorded example again to make sure you understand the correct answer.

How to Use This Book

Charts and Games

The Charts and Games begin on p. 114. The charts include Drawing Symbols, Rhythm Jumble, Terms and Symbols and Song Clue. These charts provide reinforcement for both writing and ear-training activities. Instructions on how to use each chart appear at the top of the chart.

The games include Rhythm Jumble Reading, Rhythm Jumble Solitaire, Rhythm Jumble Composer, and Mad Music. The games provide an opportunity for students to improve their facility in a fun setting.

Suggestions for Daily Ear-Training Practice

Daily practice in ear training is essential to developing total musicianship. Even if you complete your ear-training assignment immediately after your lesson, you should still do a few minutes of ear-training practice every day until your next lesson. If for some reason you finish *Sound Advice* Level 3 but have to wait before you start Level 4, you should continue to practice ear training every day.

Here are some suggestions:

Sing Intervals

One easy way to learn intervals is to relate them to the notes of the major scale. For example, to learn the perfect 5th, sing up the first five notes of a major scale, stop on the fifth note, then sing the first note again. Sing those two notes back and forth to memorize the sound of that interval.

Song clues can be helpful for identifying and singing intervals. On p. 119, there is a chart showing the ascending and descending intervals with several song clue examples. There is also space for you to add your own song clues. If you sing or hum the song clues, you will quickly memorize the sound of the intervals.

Another way to practice singing intervals is to use the Play–Hear–Sing–Play method. Follow these four steps:

1) Play the first note of the interval on your instrument.
2) Hear the second note in your mind. (Use a song clue or relate the notes to the major scale.)
3) Sing the second note out loud.
4) Play the second note on your instrument to see if you sang the right pitch.

Sing Rhythms

One of the best ways to practice rhythm is to use the music you are currently playing or singing. Choose a passage to work on, tap the beat (eventually you will *feel* the beat in your body), and play or sing the rhythms. Be sure to feel the regular accent of the time signature. Remember, the goal is to recognize the symbols on the page as familiar patterns of sounds—not to count them out. Regular practice in this manner will greatly improve your sight reading.

You can also use the Rhythm Jumble Chart on p. 115 to practice singing rhythms every day.

How to Use This Book

Play by Ear
Try to play familiar melodies on your instrument without reading from the music. To determine which note of the scale a melody starts on, sing the tune and hold the *last* note, which may well be the first note of the scale ($\hat{1}$). Now compare that last note to the first note of the melody. Are the pitches the same or different? How far apart are they? HINT: Many familiar melodies begin on the fifth scale degree ($\hat{5}$), for example, *Happy Birthday*, *Silent Night*, *Here Comes the Bride*, *Oh Christmas Tree*, and *Amazing Grace*.

Familiar Tune Dictation
Try writing out a familiar melody. To figure out the meter, sing the tune while you tap the beat and listen for the regular accents. To find which note of the scale the melody begins and ends on, use the same procedure described under Play by Ear. If you can sing the tune using pitch syllables, you should be able to write it starting on any note you choose. Compare your written version with the printed music if you have a copy.

Extra Sight Singing
You can use the Ear-Training Answer Key for extra practice in singing melodies and rhythms. When you sight sing these "answers," follow the same procedure you use when reading melodies and rhythms on the ear-training assignments.

Learning Guide

I am your Professor. I will be your guide throughout this book.

Be sure to follow my advice when I offer you a suggestion!

Review of Note Values and Rests

Here are all the note values and rests you learned in Levels 1 and 2.

Name	Symbol for Note	Number of Quarter-Note Beats	Symbol for Rest
whole note	𝑜	4	▬
half note	𝅗𝅥	2	▬
quarter note	♩	1	𝄽
eighth note	♪	$\frac{1}{2}$	
sixteenth note	𝅘𝅥𝅯	$\frac{1}{4}$	

Practice drawing rests on the Drawing Symbols Chart on p.114.

Note-Value Comparison Chart

This chart shows how all the notes relate to each other.

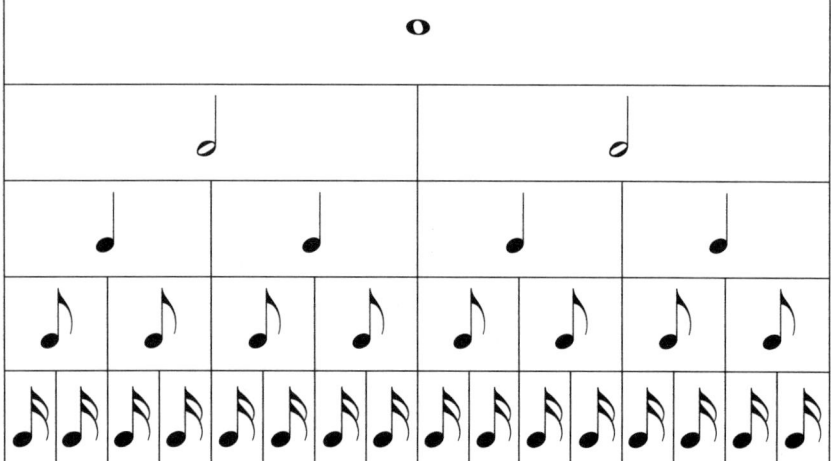

10   Lesson 1 Learning Guide   Sound Advice Level 3

Learning Guide — Lesson 1

Ties and Dots

A **tie** joins two notes together into one continuous sound. The length of the sound is equal to the total length of the two notes. In the following examples, the quarter note is equal to one beat.

For example: 𝅝 ⁀ 𝅗𝅥 = 6 beats

𝅗𝅥 ⁀ 𝅘𝅥 = 3 beats

𝅘𝅥 ⁀ 𝅘𝅥𝅮 = 1½ beats

𝅘𝅥𝅮 ⁀ 𝅘𝅥𝅯 = ¾ beat

A **dot** lengthens a note by one half of its original value.

For example:

𝅝· = 𝅝 ⁀ 𝅗𝅥
    4 + 2   = 6 beats

𝅗𝅥· = 𝅗𝅥 ⁀ 𝅘𝅥
    2 + 1   = 3 beats

𝅘𝅥· = 𝅘𝅥 ⁀ 𝅘𝅥𝅮
    1 + ½   = 1½ beats

Rhythmic Reading

Musicians "feel" the beat when they perform music. A good way to practice this skill is to tap a steady beat while you sing rhythmic patterns.

Eighth notes are pronounced "tee" and sixteenth notes are pronounced "tih."

Sing the following rhythmic units while you tap a steady quarter-note beat. Repeat each unit several times before you move on to the next one.

𝅝	𝅗𝅥·	𝅗𝅥	𝅘𝅥	𝅘𝅥𝅮𝅘𝅥𝅮	𝅘𝅥𝅯𝅘𝅥𝅯𝅘𝅥𝅯𝅘𝅥𝅯	𝅘𝅥𝅮𝅘𝅥𝅯𝅘𝅥𝅯	𝅘𝅥𝅯𝅘𝅥𝅯𝅘𝅥𝅮
Sing: ta-a-a-a	ta-a-a	ta-a	ta	ti ti	ti ka ti ka	ti ti ka	ti ka ti
Tap: x x x x	x x x	x x	x	x x	x	x	x

Sound Advice Level 3   Lesson 1 Learning Guide

LESSON 1 Learning Guide

The two units below sound exactly the same because

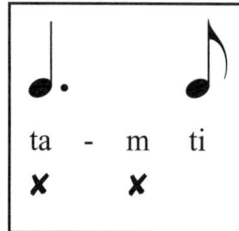

| Sing: | ta | - | m | ti | ta | - | m | ti |
| Tap: | x | | x | | x | | x | |

When you sing a rhythmic pattern, you can be silent on the rests, but you must continue to tap the quarter-note beat.

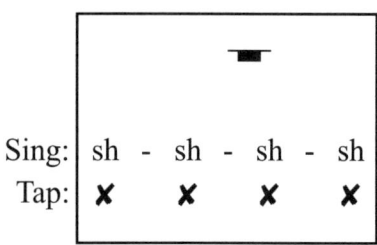 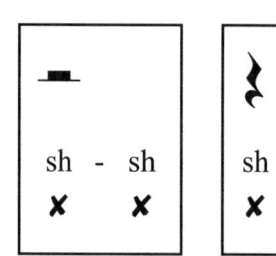

| Sing: | sh | - | sh | - | sh | - | sh | sh | - | sh | sh |
| Tap: | x | | x | | x | | x | x | | x | x |

Rhythm Jumble

On p. 115, you will find the Rhythm Jumble Chart. Each time you learn a new rhythmic unit, you will be asked to circle it on this chart.

Turn to this chart now and circle all the rhythmic units that you reviewed in this lesson:

One-Minute Rhythm Jumble

Use the Rhythm Jumble Chart to practice rhythms for *one minute* every day. Tap the quarter-note beat with your finger as you point to the rhythmic unit you are singing. Sing each unit two or three times before you move on to the next one. Gradually mix the rhythms up by randomly pointing to different units. Do this for one minute. Try not to miss a beat.

Theory Worksheet — LESSON 1

1 Complete the following chart by filling in the blanks.

12 sixteenth notes	=		eighth note(s)
4 eighth notes	=		half note(s)
2 eighth notes	=		quarter note(s)
8 sixteenth notes	=		half note(s)
3 quarter notes	=		dotted half note(s)
4 sixteenth notes	=		eighth note(s)

2 Draw a line to connect each group of notes on the left with its corresponding note value on the right.

   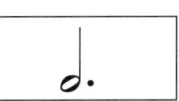

Sound Advice Level 3 — Lesson 1 Theory Worksheet — 13

LESSON 1 Theory Worksheet

3 Complete the Note-Value Comparison Chart below. The first row has been done for you.

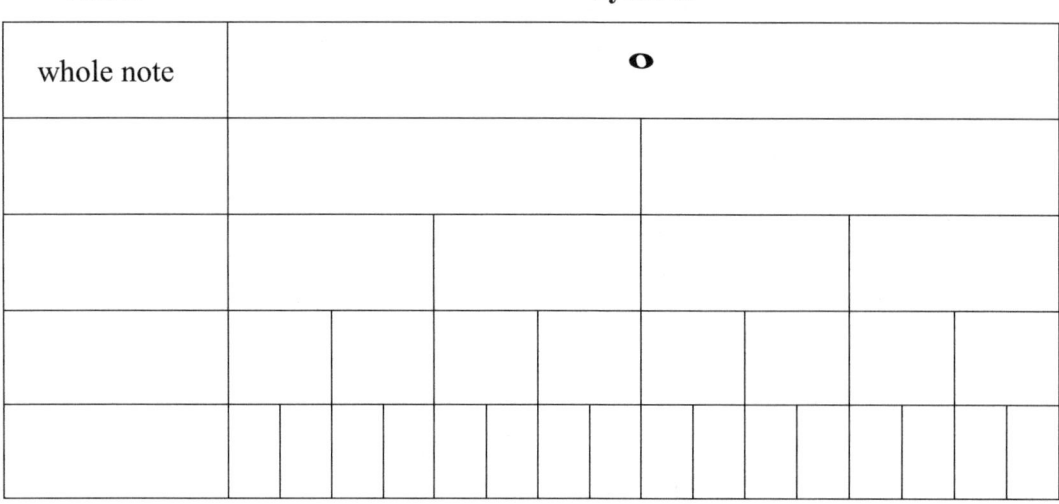

4 One-Minute Rhythm Jumble: Record the number of days you practiced. ☐

LESSON 1

Ear-Training Worksheet

Before you begin the Ear-Training Worksheets, turn to p. 7 and read the instructions.

1 Rhythmic Reading:
   a) Pause the recording. Sing the following rhythmic patterns while you tap a steady quarter-note beat.

   b) Turn to the answer key and sing along with the recording.

Sing them by yourself first. They sound the same!

2 Rhythmic Reading:
   a) Pause the recording. Sing the following rhythmic pattern while you tap a steady quarter-note beat.

   b) Turn to the answer key and sing along with the recording.

3 Rhythm Singback/Clapback: Sing, tap, or clap the rhythmic pattern you hear from memory. The pattern will be played twice but you may listen as many times as you need. Record the number of times you listened. That will be your score.

Always tap the beat while you listen

4 Rhythm Singback/Clapback: Sing, tap, or clap the rhythmic pattern you hear from memory. The pattern will be played twice but you may listen as many times as you need.

Don't forget to record your score!

5 Rhythmic Identification: Identify the correct notation for the rhythmic pattern you hear. Each pattern will be played twice.

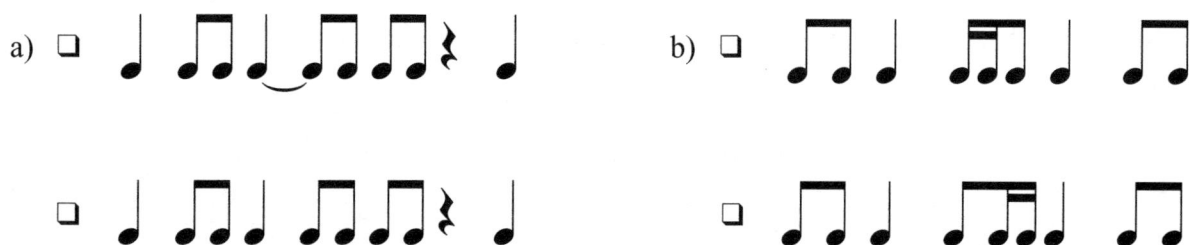

Sound Advice Level 3   Lesson 1 Ear-Training Worksheet   15

Lesson 2

Learning Guide

Half Steps and Whole Steps

Half Steps
On a keyboard, a **half step** ($\frac{1}{2}$) is the distance from one key to the very next key, whether that key is black or white. Half steps are often called **semitones**.

The two half steps that use white keys are B to C and E to F. You can use a sentence to help you remember where the white-key half steps are: for example, **B**ach **C**omposed **E**very **F**riday.

Whole Steps
A **whole step** (W) is made up of two half steps. Whole steps are often called **whole tones**. On a keyboard, there is one key between the two notes of a whole step. The key can be either black or white.

The neck of a guitar is divided into half steps by metal strips called frets. The spaces between the metal frets are also referred to as frets.

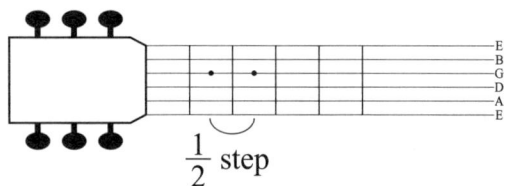

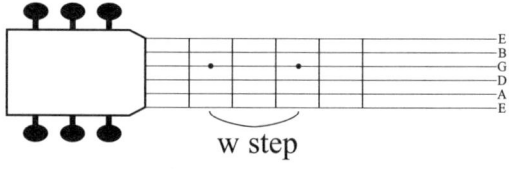

A violin does not have frets to measure the half steps. Violinists must hear exactly where to place their fingers. When playing half steps, the fingers are placed closer together than when playing half steps.

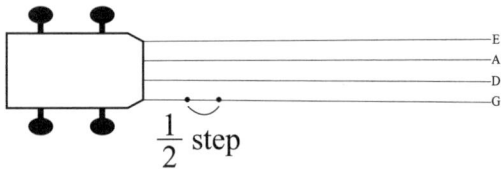

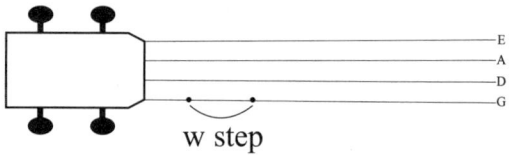

The sound of a half step or a whole step is the same on every instrument.

Learning Guide

Lesson 2

Accidentals

Accidentals are symbols that alter the pitch of a note.

A **sharp** (♯) raises the pitch of a note by one half step.

A **flat** (♭) lowers the pitch of a note by one half step.

A **natural** (♮) cancels a previous sharp or flat.

Practice drawing these symbols on p. 114.

Remember these points when you write accidentals:

- Place accidentals in *front* of a note.
- Place accidentals on the same line or space as the notehead.
- Accidentals affect *only* the pitch of the note that they are in front of. For example, a sharp on Middle C does not affect any other C on the staff.
- An accidental is cancelled by a bar line.
- If you want to cancel an accidental before the next bar line, use a natural sign.

Here are some examples of accidentals.

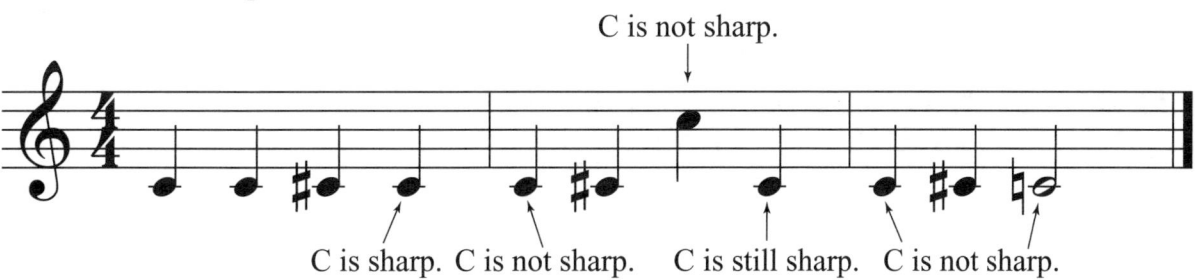

Enharmonic Equivalents

A pitch can have at least two different spellings. For example, G♯ and A♭ represent the same black key on a piano keyboard. These two notes are **enharmonic equivalents**.

G♯ or A♭

Sound Advice Level 3 — Lesson 2 Learning Guide — 17

LESSON 2: Theory Worksheet

1. On the keyboard below, draw a curved arrow from each note marked ✗ to the note a half (½) step *higher* in pitch. Write the name of the second note on the blank line. The first one has been done for you.

C# __ __ __ __ __

2. On the keyboard below, draw a curved arrow from each note marked ✗ to the note a whole (W) step *lower* in pitch. Write the name of the second note on the blank line. The first one has been done for you.

B __ __ __ __ __

3. a) Write notes to follow each accidental below.

b) Draw a line to connect each note to its corresponding key on the keyboard. The first one has been done for you.

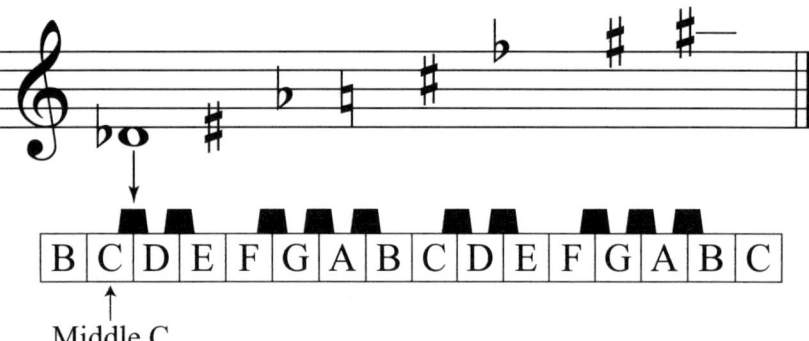

Middle C

Theory Worksheet

LESSON 2

4 Draw a line from each note on the left to its enharmonic equivalent on the right.

C	A♯
F♯	B♯
B♭	C♯
E♯	G♭
D♭	F

5 One-Minute Rhythm Jumble: Record the number of days you practiced. ☐

LESSON 2 — Ear-Training Worksheet

 1 **Editing:** Listen to the following pairs of notes. The first note of each pair will be played as you see it below. Based on what you hear, place a sharp, flat, or natural in front of the *second* note. Each pair of notes will be played twice.

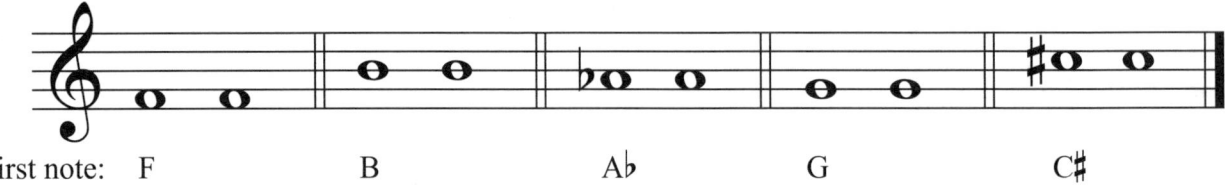

First note: F   B   A♭   G   C♯

 2 **Melodic Identification:** Identify the correct notation for the pitch pattern you hear. Each pattern will be played twice.

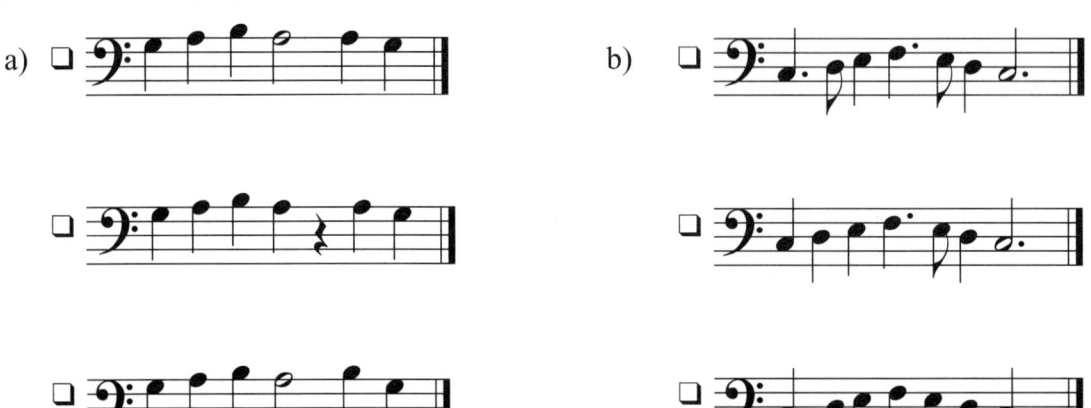

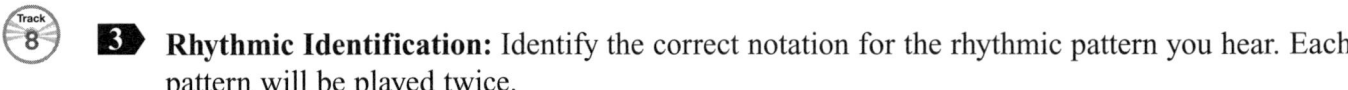 **3** **Rhythmic Identification:** Identify the correct notation for the rhythmic pattern you hear. Each pattern will be played twice.

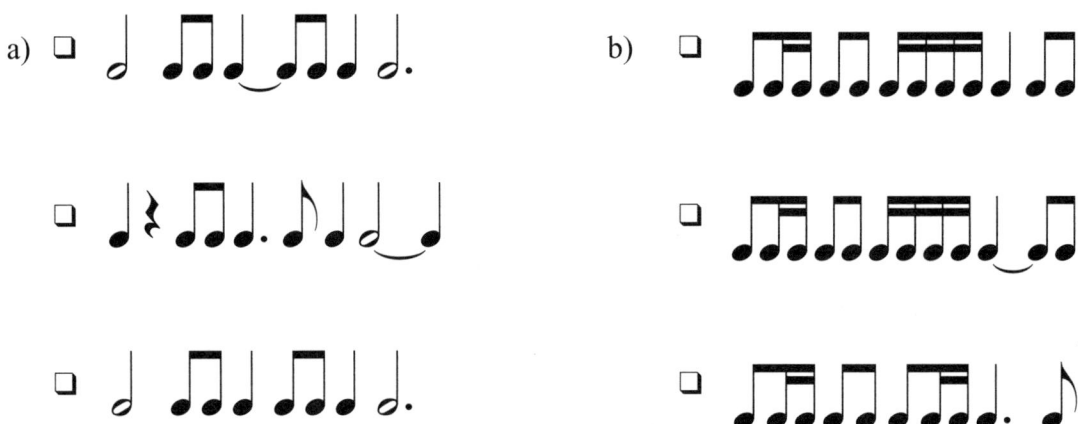

 4 **Rhythm Singback/Clapback:** Sing, tap, or clap the rhythmic pattern you hear from memory. The pattern will be played twice but you may listen as many times as you need.

I LISTENED ☐ TIMES

Learning Guide

Beaming Notes to Show the Beat

You can beam eighth notes and sixteenth notes together to show the quarter-note beat. The beams make the rhythm easier to read.

♪ ♪ are beamed like this: ♫ to show the quarter-note beat.

♬ ♬ ♬ ♬ are beamed like this: ♬♬ to show the quarter-note beat.

♪ ♬ ♬ are beamed like this: ♪♬ to show the quarter-note beat.

♬ ♬ ♪ are beamed like this: ♬♪ to show the quarter-note beat.

All the notes on the Rhythm Jumble Chart on p. 115 are beamed to show the quarter-note beat.

Circling the Beat

In Level 3, the beat is always based on the quarter note. In your Theory Worksheets, you will often be asked to circle the quarter-note beats. Use these points as a guide:

- If all the notes in a quarter-note beat have flags, they are beamed together. Circle them like this:

- Circle quarter notes and quarter rests like this:

- The rhythmic unit of a dotted quarter plus an eighth note has two quarter-note beats. Circle them like this:

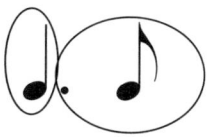

- For notes or rests that are larger than a quarter note, draw a bigger circle. Write the equivalent number of quarter notes inside the circle, like this:

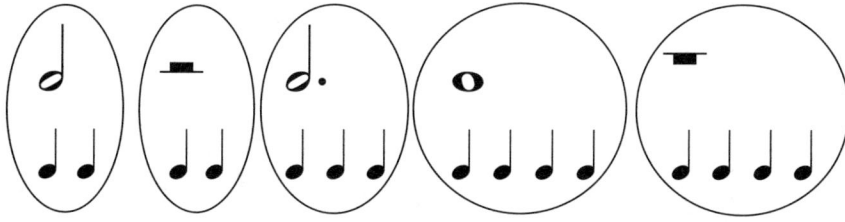

Sound Advice Level 3   Lesson 3 Learning Guide   21

LESSON 3 Learning Guide

Rhythmic Dictation

Writing down–or notating—what you hear is called dictation. When you do rhythmic dictation, you only write the rhythm, even if the example you hear is a melody.

You may be asked to write a rhythmic pattern as you listen to it, or to memorize the pattern first and then write it down from memory. If you have memorized the pattern, you can sing it to yourself as you write it down.

Follow these steps when you do either kind of rhythmic dictation.

Try this example:

1 Write a stem for each sound you hear. Write the stems close together when you hear short notes, and farther apart when you hear longer notes.

2 Sing the pattern back to yourself from memory while you follow the stems you have written. Try to remember which notes were longer and which were shorter. Here, you can add the notehead for a half note where you heard the longer note. Draw beams to join the shorter notes.

3 Add noteheads to the other stems to complete your dictation. If you are not working from memory, you may need to listen to the pattern several more times.

Theory Worksheet — Lesson 3

1 Rewrite the following example, adding beams to the eighth notes and sixteenth notes to show the quarter-note beat.

Rewrite here:

2 Circle the quarter-note beats in the following rhythmic pattern.

3 On the keyboard below, draw a curved arrow from each note marked ✘ to the note a whole (W) step *lower* in pitch. Write the name of the second note on the blank line. The first one has been done for you.

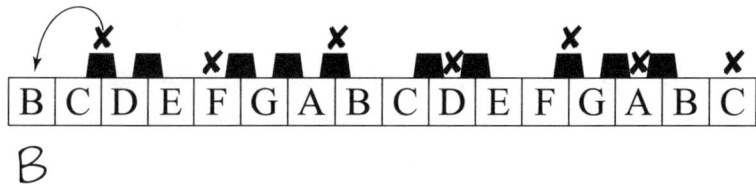

B __ __ __ __ __ __

4 On the keyboard below, draw a curved arrow from each note marked ✘ to the note a half step ($\frac{1}{2}$) step *higher* in pitch. Write the name of the second note on the blank line. The first one has been done for you.

C __ __ __ __ __ __

5 Create whole steps by adding any necessary accidentals to the *second* note.

6 Create half steps by adding any necessary accidentals to the *second* note.

7 One-Minute Rhythm Jumble: Record the number of days you practiced. ☐

LESSON 3
Ear-Training Worksheet

1) Rhythmic Reading:
 a) Pause the recording. Sing the following rhythmic pattern while you tap a steady quarter-note beat.

 b) Turn to the answer key and sing along with the recording.

2) Rhythmic Identification: Identify the correct notation for the rhythmic pattern you hear. Each example will be played twice.

a) ☐    b) ☐

☐    ☐

☐    ☐

3) Rhythm Singback/Clapback: Sing, tap, or clap the rhythmic pattern you hear from memory. The pattern will be played twice.

4) Rhythmic Dictation: Write the rhythmic pattern you hear in the space below. Listen to the example as many times as you need. The pattern will be played twice.

Write it down as you hear it!

5) Editing: Listen to the following pairs of notes. The first note of each pair will be played as you see it below. Based on what you hear, place a sharp, flat, or natural in front of the *second* note. Each pair of notes will be played twice.

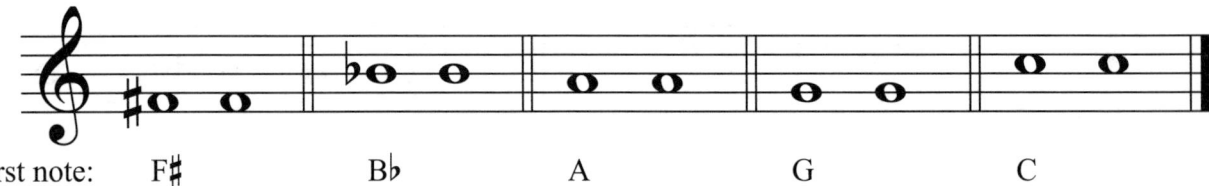

First note: F♯   B♭   A   G   C

24   Lesson 3 Ear-Training Worksheet   Sound Advice Level 3

Learning Guide

Meter and Time Signatures

A repeating pattern of strong and weak beats is called **meter**. A **time signature** shows the meter of a piece of music.

A time signature is written at the beginning of a piece. When the pattern of regular beats changes in the middle of a piece of music, a new time signature is needed.

The top number of a time signature tells you the number of beats in each measure—that is, the type of meter. The bottom number of a time signature tells you what kind of note gets one beat.

When a time signature has two beats in each measure, the meter is **duple**.

The accent pattern for duple meter is "**strong**–weak."

When a time signature has three beats in each measure, the meter is **triple**.

The accent pattern for triple meter is "**strong**–weak–weak."

A time signature should never look like a fraction!

When a time signature has four beats in each measure, the meter is **quadruple**.

The accent pattern for quadruple meter is "**strong**–weak–medium–weak."

$\frac{4}{4}$ is also called **common time**.

The symbol for common time is **C**.

On the grand staff, the time signature must appear on both staffs.

Gavotta

James Hook
(1746–1827)

Source: *New Guida di Musica* (1796)

LESSON 4 Theory Worksheet

1 Circle the quarter-note beats, then add the time signature to the following excerpt.

Musette
BWV Anh. 126

Anon.

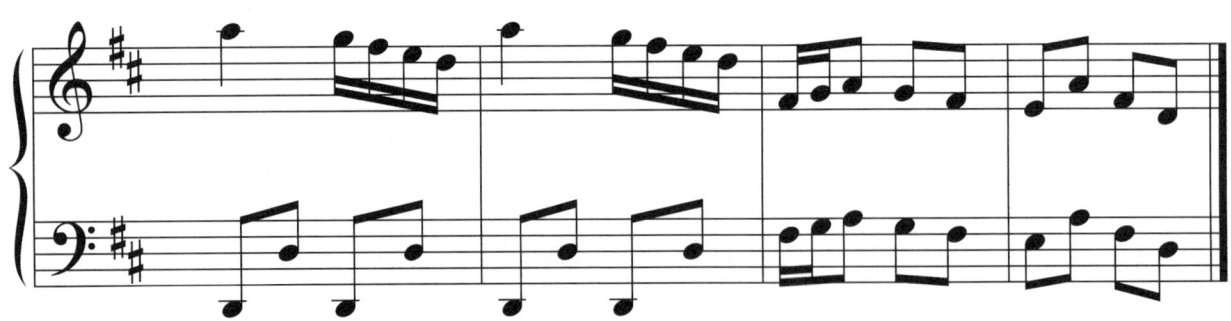

2 Circle the quarter-note beats in the following melody.
Add the time signature and write the accent pattern above each measure.

3 Circle the quarter-note beats. Add bar lines according to the time signature.

a)

b)

Don't forget to use double bar lines at the end!

4 Draw a line to connect each note on the left with its enharmonic equivalent on the right.

B♯		C♯
D♭		G♭
F♯		B♭
F♭		C
A♯		E

5 One-Minute Rhythm Jumble: Record the number of days you practiced. ☐

LESSON 4
Ear-Training Worksheet

Beginning with this lesson, the instructions will no longer be read aloud on the recording. Be sure to read each question carefully before you listen.

Read carefully!

1. Rhythmic Reading:
a) Pause the recording. Sing the following rhythmic pattern while you tap a steady quarter-note beat.

b) Turn to the answer key and sing along with the recording.

2. Rhythm Singback/Clapback: Sing, tap, or clap the rhythmic pattern you hear from memory.

3. Rhythmic Dictation: Write the rhythmic pattern you hear in the space below. Listen to the example as many times as you need. The rhythm is in 2/4 time and will require bar lines.

Write it down as you hear it!

4. Meter Identification: Identify the meter of the following examples as duple or triple.

a) ❑ duple   b) ❑ duple
   ❑ triple   ❑ triple

Tap the beat as you listen!

5. Editing: Listen to the following pairs of notes. The first note of each pair will be played as you see it below. Based on what you hear, write a sharp, flat, or natural in front of the *second* note.

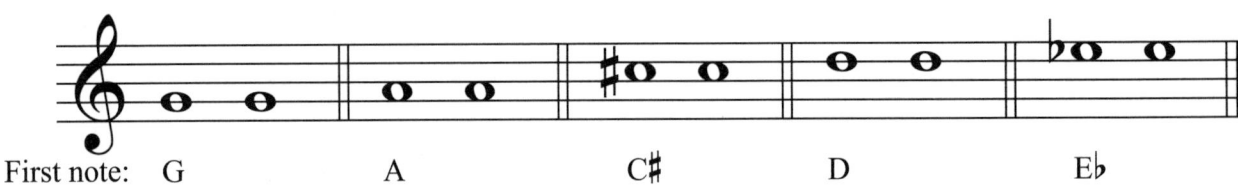

First note: G   A   C♯   D   E♭

Major Scale Review: C, G, D, and F Major

Major scales can start on any note. All major scales have a similar sound because of the pattern of whole steps and half steps:

W W ½ W W W ½

Here are the scales you have learned so far:

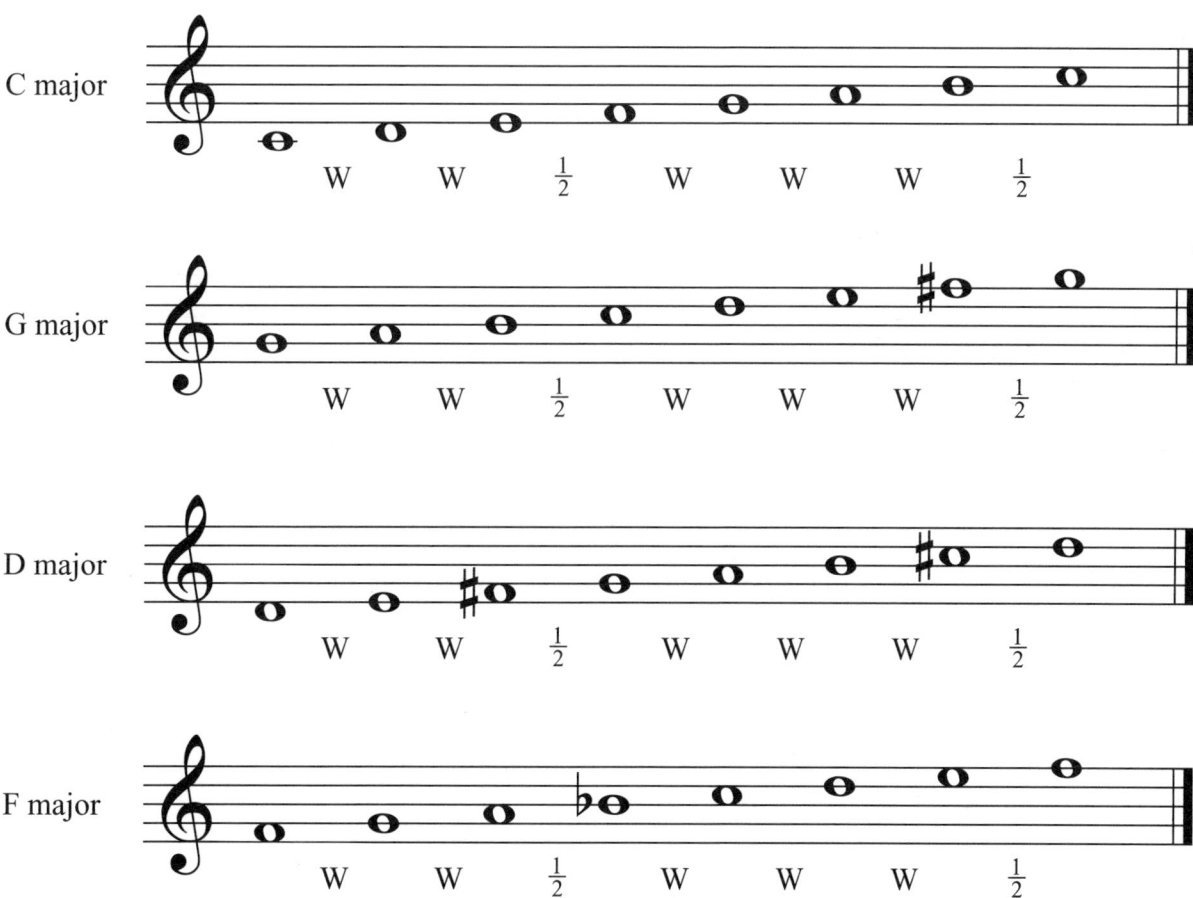

The scales that start on G, D, and F need accidentals to maintain the pattern of whole steps and half steps.

Scale Degree Numbers

Each scale tone has a number. A carat sign (^) above the number identifies that number as a **scale degree**. The first note of a scale is always $\hat{1}$ no matter where it is placed in the octave.

LESSON 5 Learning Guide

The B♭ Major Scale

For a major scale starting on B♭, you need B♭ and E♭ to maintain the pattern of whole steps and half steps.

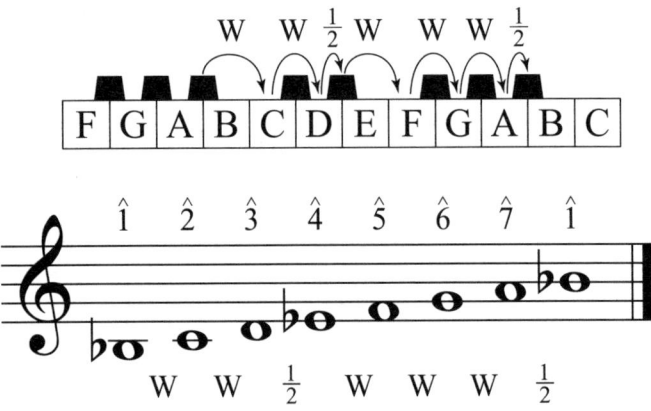

Sight Singing

The best way to learn the sound of the major scale is to sing it out loud. We recommend using pitch syllables when you sing scales and melodies.

do re mi fa sol la ti do ti la sol fa mi re do

Your teacher may suggest a different method for sight singing. For a description of the most common sight-singing syllable systems, see p. 150.

Theory Worksheet

LESSON 5

1. Draw curved arrows on the keyboard below to create a B♭ major scale. The first arrow has been drawn for you. When you are finished, play the scale you have written.

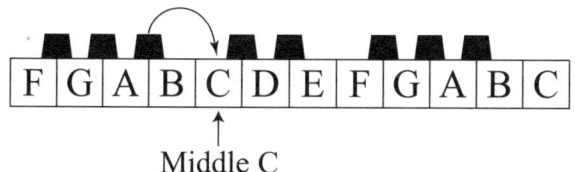

Middle C

2. Using the keyboard above as a guide, write a B♭ major scale on the staff below. Use accidentals.

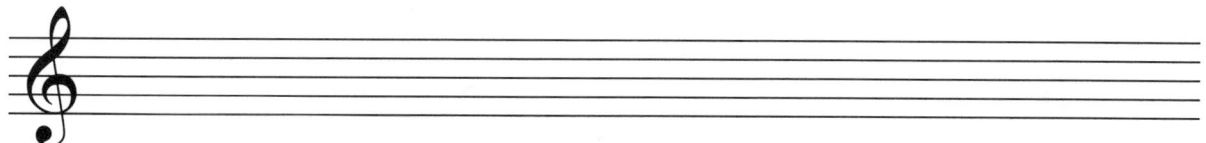

3. Draw curved arrows on the keyboard below to create a D major scale. The first arrow has been done for you. When you are finished, play the scale you have written.

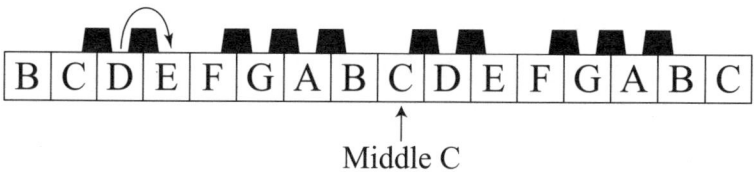

Middle C

4. Using the keyboard above as a guide, write a D major scale on the staff below. Use accidentals.

5. Circle the quarter-note beats. Add bar lines according to the time signature.

6. One-Minute Rhythm Jumble: Record the number of days you practiced.

LESSON 5: Ear-Training Worksheet

Track 20 **1) Sight Singing:**
a) Pause the recording. Sing the C major scale, ascending and descending.
b) Turn to the answer key and sing along with the recording.

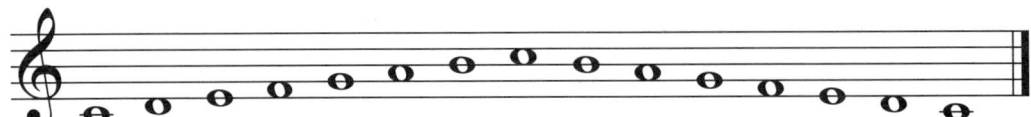

Track 21 **2) Sight Singing:**
a) Pause the recording. Sing the following melody while you tap a steady quarter-note beat.
b) Turn to the answer key and sing along with the recording.

Track 22 **3) Editing:**
a) Add ties where you hear them in the following rhythmic pattern.
a) Sing the edited rhythmic pattern while you tap a steady beat. The pattern will be played twice but you may listen as many times as you need.

Add ties!

Track 23 **4) Rhythmic Dictation:** Write the rhythmic pattern you hear in the space below. Listen to the example as many times as you need. The rhythm is in 3/4 time and will require bar lines.

Write it down as you hear it!

Track 24 **5) Meter Identification:** Identify the meter of the examples you hear as duple or triple.

a) ☐ duple   b) ☐ duple
   ☐ triple   ☐ triple

Tap the beat as you listen!

32 — Lesson 5 Ear-Training Worksheet — Sound Advice Level 3

Learning Guide

Key Signatures

When a piece of music uses the notes from a particular scale, it is said to be in the **key** of that scale. For example, the melody in Example 1 uses notes of the B♭ major scale. Therefore, it is in the key of B♭ major.

The accidentals in this melody are the ones needed for the B♭ major scale.

Ex. 1

The accidentals needed for the key of a piece can be grouped at the beginning of each line of music as a **key signature**. Example 2 shows the melody from Example 1 written with a key signature instead of accidentals. The key signature for B♭ major has two flats because the scale of B♭ major has two flats.

Ex. 2

Remember these points when you write key signatures on the staff:

- The key signature always goes *before* the time signature.
- On the grand staff, the key signature appears in both clefs.
- The sharps or flats in a key signature affect all pitches with that letter name. For example, a B♭ in the key signature means that *all* B's are played as B♭.
- The sharps or flats in a key signature are always in the same order and position on the staff.
- When you use a key signature, you do not need to write accidentals in front of the notes.

Study the arrangement of sharps and flats in the following key signatures.

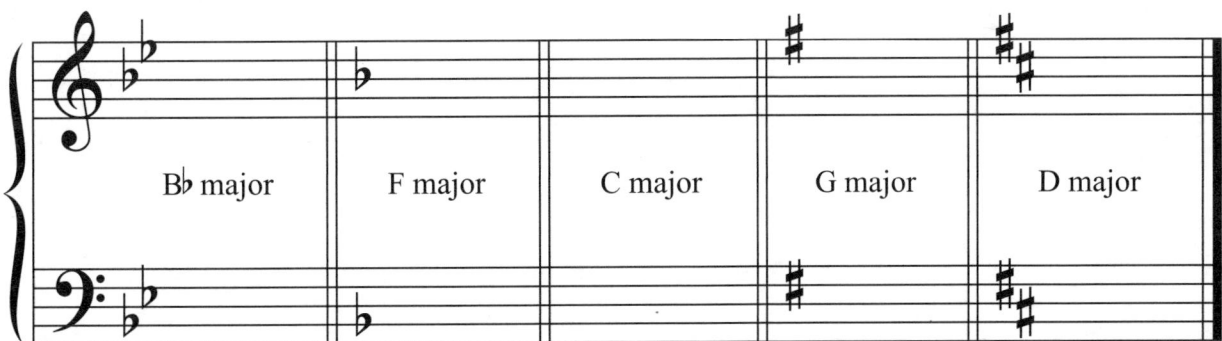

Sound Advice Level 3   Lesson 6 Learning Guide   33

LESSON 6 Theory Worksheet

1 Write the pattern of whole steps and half steps in a major scale.

___ ___ ___ ___ ___ ___ ___

2 Draw curved arrows on the keyboard below to create an F major scale.

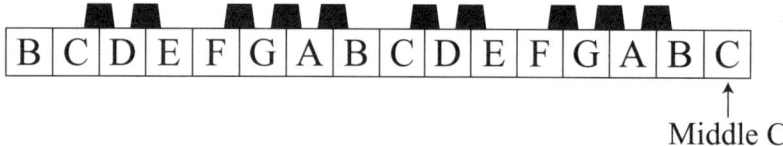

3 Using the keyboard above as a guide, write an F major scale on the staff. Write whole notes and use a key signature instead of accidentals.

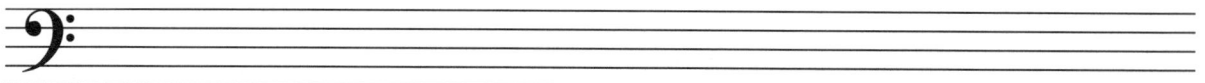

4 Draw curved arrows on the keyboard below to create a G major scale.

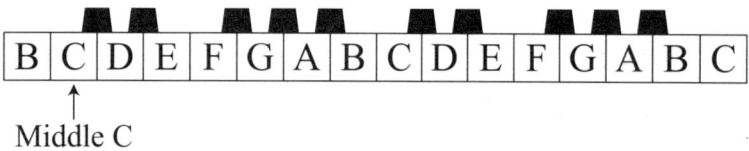

5 Using the keyboard above as a guide, write a G major scale on the staff. Write whole notes and use a key signature instead of accidentals.

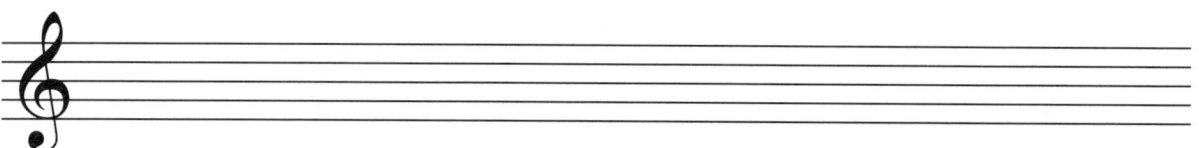

6 Write the following key signatures on the grand staff below.

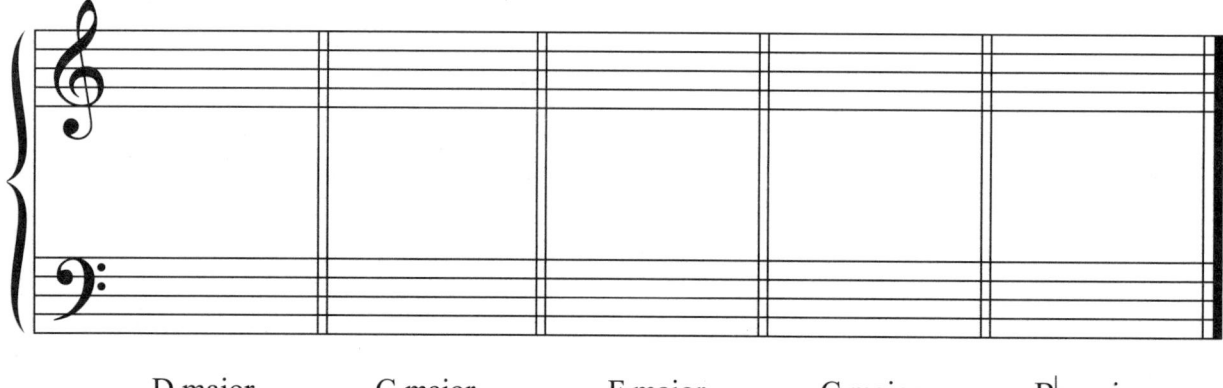

D major   G major   F major   C major   B♭ major

7 One-Minute Rhythm Jumble: Record the number of days you practiced. ☐

LESSON 6

Ear-Training Worksheet

 1 **Sight Singing:**

a) Pause the recording. Sing the B♭ major scale, ascending and descending.

b) Turn to the answer key and sing along with the recording.

 2 **Sight Singing:**

a) Pause the recording. Sing the following melody while you tap a steady quarter-note beat.

b) Turn to the answer key and sing along with the recording.

 3 **Melody Singback/Playback:** Sing the melody you hear from memory, then play it on your instrument. The melody is in F major, in 3/4 time. The melody will be played twice.

 4 **Rhythm Singback/Clapback:** Sing, tap, or clap the rhythmic pattern you hear from memory.

 5 **Rhythmic Dictation:** Write the rhythmic pattern you hear in the space below. Listen to the example as many times as you need. The rhythm is in 2/4 time.

Write it down as you hear it.

 6 **Editing:**

a) Add ties where you hear them in the following melody.

b) Sing the edited melody while you tap a steady quarter-note beat.

Sound Advice Level 3   Lesson 6 Ear-Training Worksheet   35

Learning Guide

Naming Intervals

An **interval** is the distance between two notes. The name of an interval tells you two things: the *size* (shown with a number) and the *quality* (shown with a word: major, minor, or perfect).

To identify the size and quality of an interval:

1) Count the distance from one note to the other. Include both the lowest and the highest note in the total.

2) Identify the scale that begins on the lower note (in this case, C major). Think in this key.

3) Determine whether the upper note also belongs to this key. Intervals that belong to the major key of the bottom note are named as follows:

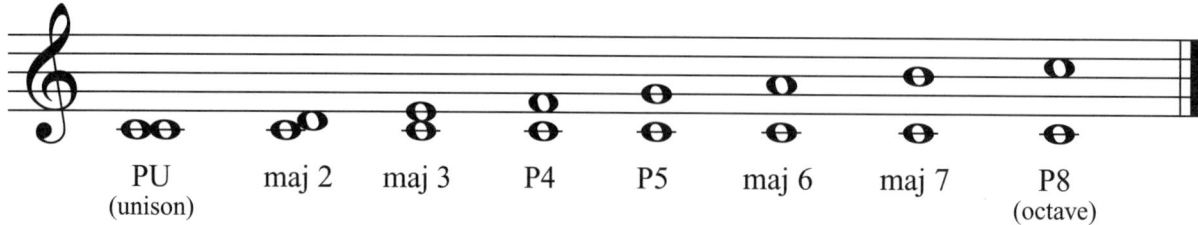

Unisons, 4ths, 5ths, and 8ves are **perfect** intervals. Perfect intervals are symbolized with a "P" and the size of the interval: PU, P4, P5, and P8. (HINT: Look at the Professor's license plate number!)

The other intervals—2nds, 3rds, 6ths, and 7ths—are **major** intervals. Major intervals are symbolized with "maj" and the size of the interval: maj 2, maj 3, maj 6, maj 7.

Naming Minor Intervals

When the upper note of a major interval is lowered by a half step, the quality of the interval changes from major to minor. Minor intervals are symbolized with "min" and the size of the interval: min 2, min 3, min 6, min 7.

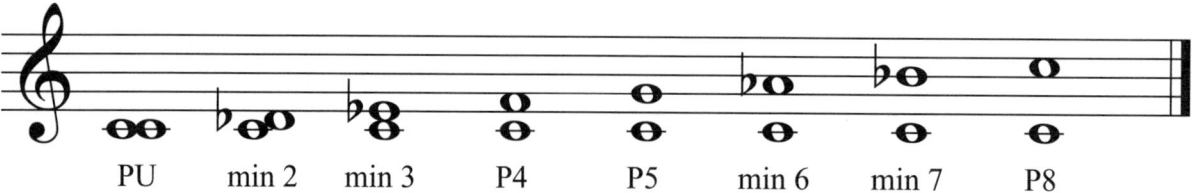

When you are asked to name an interval, you need to know three things:

1) the size of the interval
2) the major scale that starts on the bottom note
3) the quality of the interval

Learning Guide

Lesson 7

Here are some examples:

1) What size is this interval? __6__
2) What major scale begins on the bottom note? __F major__
3) What is the quality of this interval? __major__ (D is the 6th note of the F major scale)

Interval name: __maj 6__

1) What size is this interval? __6__
2) What major scale begins on the bottom note? __F major__
3) What is the quality of this interval? __minor__ (D♭ does not belong to the F major scale—it is a half step lower.)

Interval name: __min 6__

The Sound of the Major 2nd, Major 3rd, and Perfect 5th

To memorize the sound of the major 2nd, major 3rd, and perfect 5th, sing up from the first note of a major scale, and then repeat the lowest and highest notes.

Sing: do re   do re

Sing: do re mi   do mi

Sing: do re mi fa sol   do sol

You might find it helpful to relate the sound of an interval to a familiar melody. Here are some examples for the major 2nd, major 3rd, and perfect 5th.

major 2nd	Are You Sleeping? (Frère Jacques) Yankee Doodle
major 3rd	Oh, When the Saints Go Marching In For He's a Jolly Good Fellow
perfect 5th	Theme from Star Wars Twinkle, Twinkle, Little Star

The Song Clue Chart on p. 119 lists song clues for all the intervals that are covered in Level 3. There is also a column for you to add your own clues.

Each time you review an interval or learn a new one, put a ✔ beside that interval on the Song Clue Chart. Do this for the major 2nd, major 3rd, and perfect 5th.

For additional ear-training practice tips, see "Suggestions for Daily Ear-Training Practice" on p. 8.

LESSON 7 Theory Worksheet

1 For each interval below, answer the questions and write the full name of the interval.

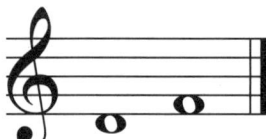

What size is this interval? _____
What major scale begins on the bottom note? _____
What quality is this interval? _____
Interval name: _____

What size is this interval? _____
What major scale begins on the bottom note? _____
What quality is this interval? _____
Interval name: _____

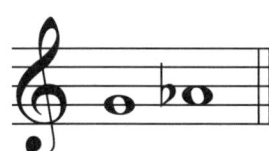

What size is this interval? _____
What major scale begins on the bottom note? _____
What quality is this interval? _____
Interval name: _____

What size is this interval? _____
What major scale begins on the bottom note? _____
What quality is this interval? _____
Interval name: _____

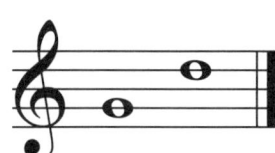

What size is this interval? _____
What major scale begins on the bottom note? _____
What quality is this interval? _____
Interval name: _____

2 Draw a line to connect each group of notes on the left with its corresponding note value on the right.

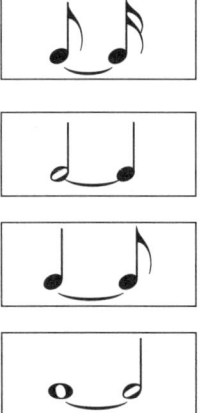
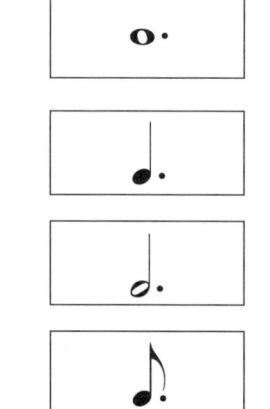

38   Lesson 7 Theory Worksheet   Sound Advice Level 3

Theory Worksheet — Lesson 7

3 Complete the following chart by filling in each blank with one *dotted* note.

𝅘𝅥	+	♪	=	
𝅝	+	𝅗𝅥	=	
♪	+	𝅘𝅥𝅮 (sixteenth)	=	
𝅗𝅥	+	𝅘𝅥	=	

4 Complete the following chart by writing the correct number in the empty box. Refer to the Note-Value Comparison Chart in Lesson 1 if you need help.

A dotted half note	=		quarter notes
A dotted eighth note	=		sixteenth notes
A dotted quarter note	=		eighth notes
A dotted whole note	=		half notes

5 Complete the following chart by filling in each blank with *one* note.

♪	+		=	♪.
𝅗𝅥	+		=	𝅗𝅥.
𝅝	+		=	𝅝.
𝅘𝅥	+		=	𝅘𝅥.

6 One-Minute Rhythm Jumble: Record the number of days you practiced. ☐

LESSON 7 — Ear-Training Worksheet

 1 **Sight Singing:**

a) Pause the recording. Sing the following F major scale, ascending and descending.

b) Turn to the answer key and sing along with the recording.

 2 **Sight Singing:**

a) Pause the recording. Sing the following melody while you tap a steady quarter-note beat.

b) Turn to the answer key and sing along with the recording.

 3 **Interval Identification:** Identify the intervals you hear as maj 2, maj 3, or P5.

a)   b)   c)   d)   e)   f)   g)

 4 **Rhythm Clapback:** Clap the *rhythm* of the melody you hear from memory. Your goal is to memorize the rhythm after the melody has been played twice. Record the number of times you listened.

 5 **Melody Singback/Playback:** Sing the melody you hear from memory, then play it on your instrument. The melody is in the key of C major, in 3/4 time.

Learning Guide — Lesson 8

Incomplete Measures

The first beat of a measure is called the **downbeat**. You can feel the strong accent on this beat.

Some melodies begin on the downbeat. Other melodies begin on an unaccented note (or notes). An unaccented note at the beginning of a phrase is called an **upbeat** or a **pickup**. It can also be called an **anacrusis**.

If a melody begins on an upbeat, both the first measure and the last measure will be incomplete. The melody below is in 3/4 time. It begins on the third beat, which is a weak beat. The first note of the melody is a quarter-note upbeat.

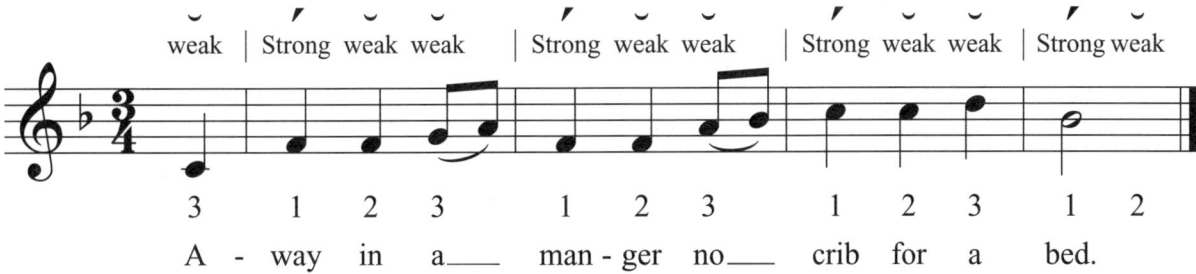

Take a close look at the first and last measures of this melody. Both measures are incomplete. The "missing" third beat of the last measure is equal to the upbeat that begins the melody. Together these two incomplete measures add up to one full measure. No rests are needed to complete these measures.

Scale Degree Names

The first note of a scale—$\hat{1}$—is called the **tonic**. Think of tonic as the "home note." When a melody ends on the tonic, it sounds "finished"—as if the tune has come home. The tonic note at the end of a melody is usually approached by a step from above or below.

In a major scale, the seventh scale degree—$\hat{7}$—is called the **leading note**. The leading note is only a half step below the tonic. Think of $\hat{7}$—the leading note—as "leading" the way "home" ($\hat{7}$ to $\hat{1}$, or ti–do).

The fifth note of a scale—$\hat{5}$—is called the **dominant**. When a melody begins with an upbeat, the first note is often the dominant. Here is an example.

Tonic – the first scale degree ($\hat{1}$ or do)
Dominant – the fifth scale degree ($\hat{5}$ or sol)
Leading note – the seventh scale degree ($\hat{7}$ or ti)

LESSON 8 Learning Guide

The Sound of the Perfect 4th

To memorize the sound of a perfect 4th (P4), you can sing up the major scale from $\hat{1}$ to $\hat{4}$ (do to fa), then repeat $\hat{1}$ and $\hat{4}$, as shown below.

Sing: do re mi fa do fa

However, most melodies that begin with an ascending perfect 4th actually begin on the dominant—the fifth note of the scale ($\hat{5}$).

To find this interval, sing the following exercise:

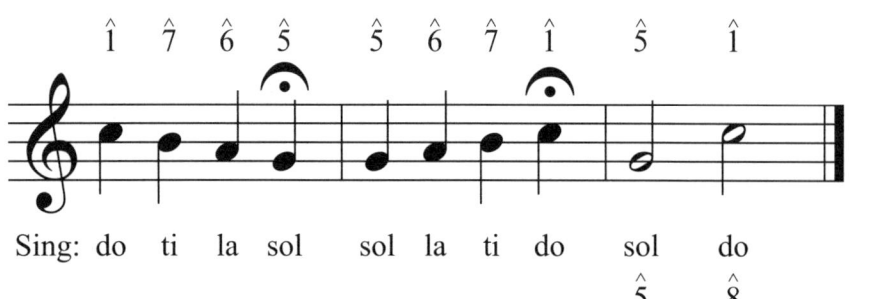

Sing: do ti la sol sol la ti do sol do

Review the Terms and Symbols Chart on pp. 117–118.

The distance between $\hat{5}$ and $\hat{1}$ (sol and do) is a perfect 4th. It often occurs as an upbeat, as in the following melody.

sol do

Many melodies begin with an ascending perfect 4th from $\hat{5}$ up to $\hat{1}$. Turn to the Song Clue Chart on p. 119 and put a ✔ beside the perfect 4th (ascending).

LESSON 8

Theory Worksheet

1 For each interval below, answer the questions and write the full name of the interval.

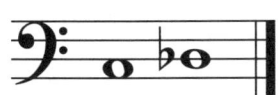
What size is this interval? _____
What major scale begins on the bottom note? _____
What quality is this interval? _____
Interval name: _____

What size is this interval? _____
What major scale begins on the bottom note? _____
What quality is this interval? _____
Interval name: _____

What size is this interval? _____
What major scale begins on the bottom note? _____
What quality is this interval? _____
Interval name: _____

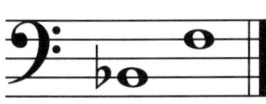
What size is this interval? _____
What major scale begins on the bottom note? _____
What quality is this interval? _____
Interval name: _____

What size is this interval? _____
What major scale begins on the bottom note? _____
What quality is this interval? _____
Interval name: _____

2 For the following melody:
a) Name the key.

b) Write the accent pattern above each measure.

c) Circle and label the tonic (T), the dominant (D), and the leading note (LN). (Scale degrees may occur more than once.)

Key: _____

3 One-Minute Rhythm Jumble: Record the number of days you practiced. ☐

LESSON 8

Ear-Training Worksheet

 1 **Sight Singing:**
   a) Pause the recording. Sing the D major scale, ascending and descending.
   b) Turn to the answer key and sing along with the recording.

 2 **Sight Singing:**
   a) Pause the recording. Sing the following melody while you tap a steady quarter-note beat.
   b) Turn to the answer key and sing along with the recording.

 3 **Interval Identification:** Identify the intervals you hear as maj 2, maj 3, P4, or P5.

   a)   b)   c)   d)   e)   f)   g)

 4 **Interval Identification:** The first note of each interval is given. Name the interval you hear and write the second note. Each interval will be played twice.

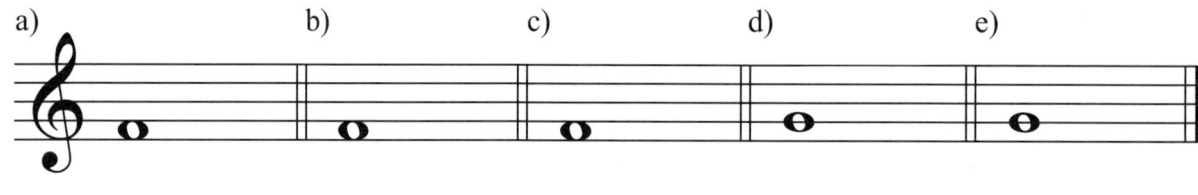

 5 **Rhythmic Dictation:** Write the rhythmic pattern you hear in the space below. Listen as many times as you need. The rhythm is in $\frac{3}{4}$ time.

Write it down as you hear it!

Major and Minor 2nds: A Shortcut

You have learned to identify intervals by relating them to a major key and scale. In the first example below, the distance from F to G is a 2nd. This interval is a major 2nd because G (the upper note) belongs to the major scale that starts on F (the lower note). The second example is also a 2nd, but G♭ does not belong to the scale of F major. Because G♭ is a half step lower than the second note of the F major scale, this interval is a minor 2nd.

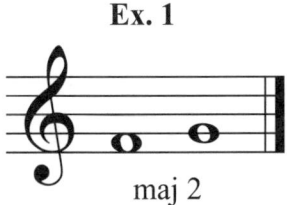

In Level 2, you learned this shortcut to identify the quality of a 2nd as major or minor.

- Major 2nds are always whole steps (W).

- Minor 2nds are always half steps ($\frac{1}{2}$).

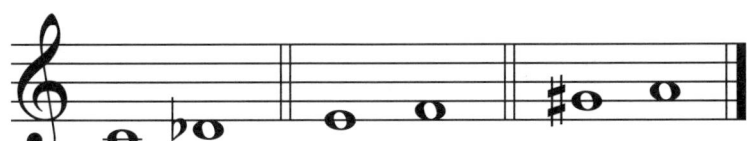

Mad Music Game: Name the 2nds

This timed interval-reading game uses the interval sheet on p. 121. The goal is to name all the intervals on a sheet in two minutes or less. Once you can name all the major and minor 2nds within two minutes, you will have earned the status of "2nds Expert" for Level 3 and will be awarded a Certificate of Achievement (on the inside back cover).

The easiest way to play Mad Music is to have someone follow the answer sheet while you name the 2nds out loud. Beginning with Lesson 9, you will often be asked to record three Mad Music scores on your Theory Worksheet. This means that part of your homework assignment for that lesson is to play Mad Music at least three times. Once you have mastered the interval sheet, you do not have to record any more Mad Music scores.

Lesson 9 Learning Guide

The Sound of the Minor 2nd

You can learn to recognize the sound of a minor 2nd by singing a major 2nd followed by a minor 2nd. You may use the pitch syllables shown below.

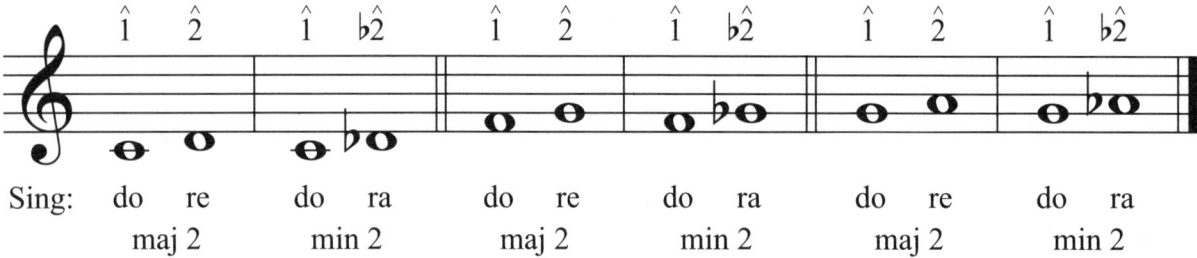

Another way to learn the sound of this interval is to play a major 2nd on your instrument, then lower the top note by a half step to create a minor 2nd. Listen for the difference in sound.

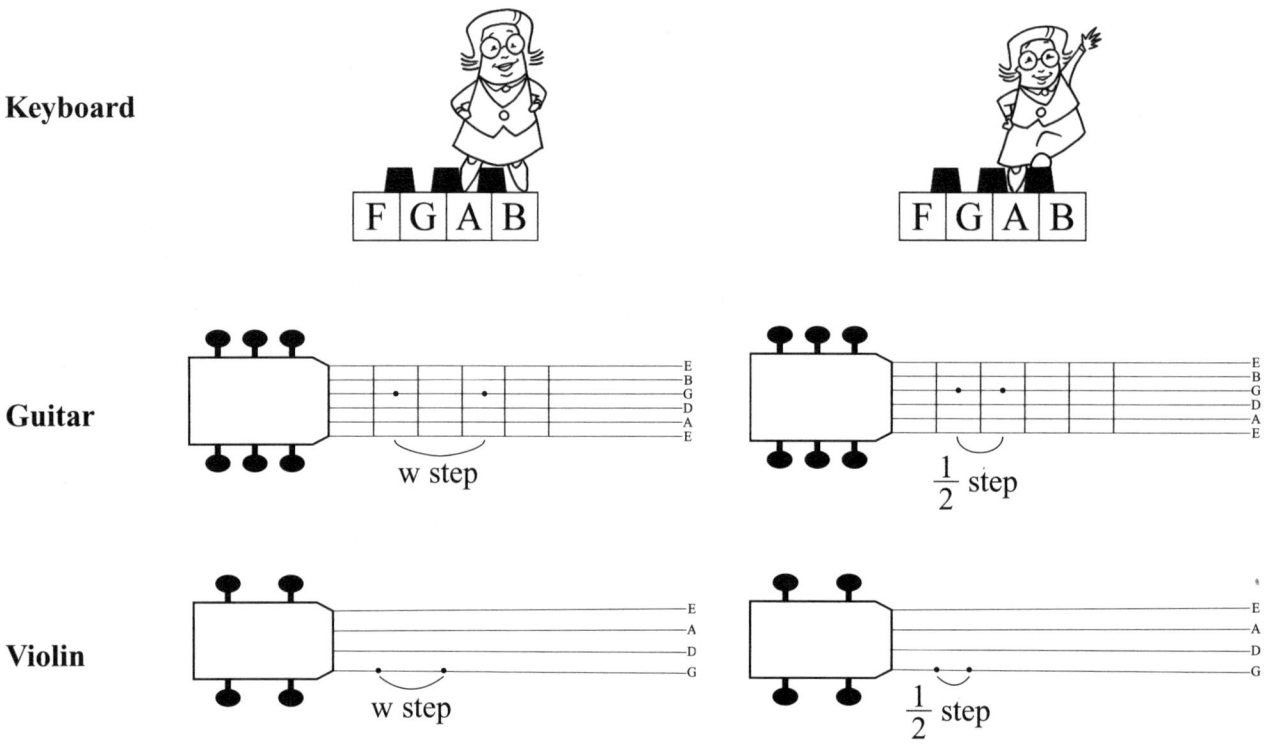

Sing the following melody, and listen closely to the sound of the last two notes. The leading note ($\hat{7}$ or ti) moving up to the tonic ($\hat{1}$ or do) makes a minor 2nd.

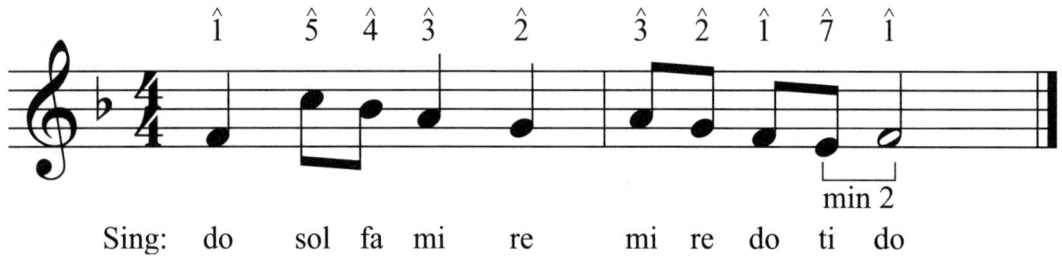

Minor 2nds are often found at the end of songs, but few songs begin with this interval. Turn to the Song Clue Chart on p. 119 and put a ✔ beside the minor 2nd (min 2).

LESSON 9

Theory Worksheet

1 Draw a line to connect each note on the left with its enharmonic equivalent on the right.

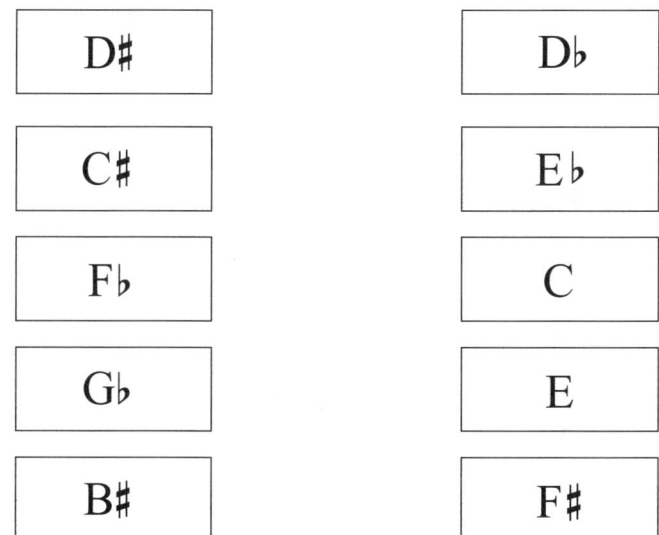

2 Turn each major 2nd into a minor 2nd by writing an accidental in front of the *upper* note.

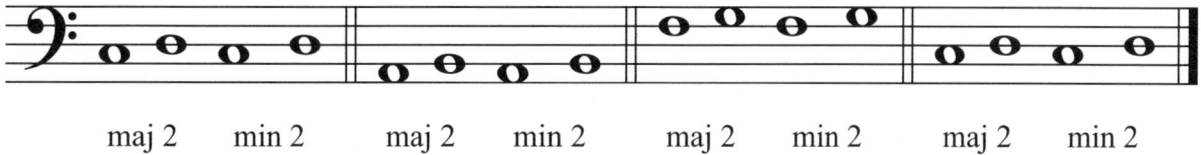

maj 2   min 2   maj 2   min 2   maj 2   min 2   maj 2   min 2

3 a) Identify the following intervals as whole steps or half steps by circling W or $\frac{1}{2}$ above the staff.

b) Name the intervals as major 2nds or minor 2nds. The first one has been done for you.

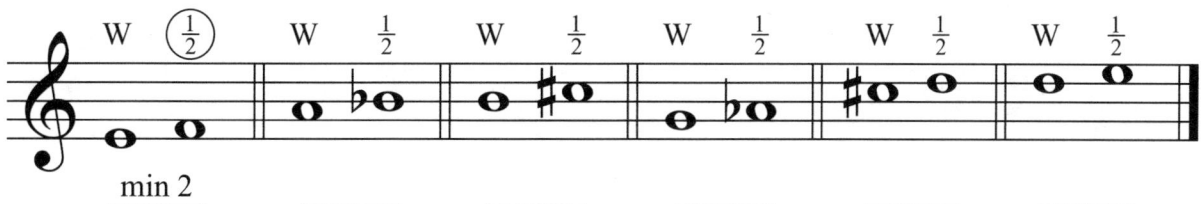

min 2

4 Circle the quarter-note beats, then add the time signature to each of the following rhythms.

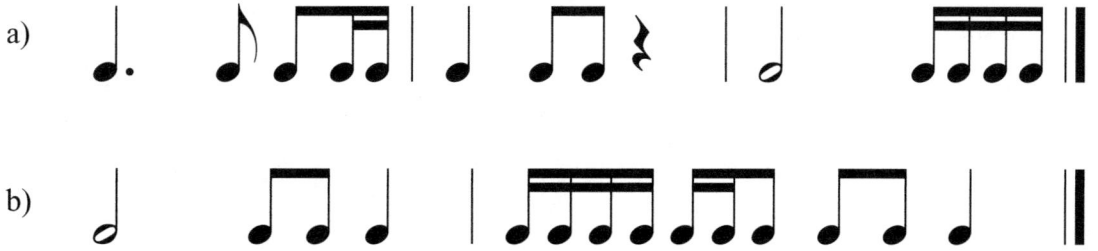

5 Mad Music Scores

LESSON 9 Ear-Training Worksheet

1 Sight Singing:
   a) Pause the recording. Sing the following melody while you tap a steady quarter-note beat.
   b) Turn to the answer key and sing along with the recording.

2 Interval Identification: Identify the intervals you hear as min 2 or maj 2.

a)   b)   c)   d)   e)   f)   g)

3 Editing: The following intervals are written as major 2nds. If you hear a major 2nd, leave the interval as written. If you hear a minor 2nd, write the appropriate accidental in front of the upper note.

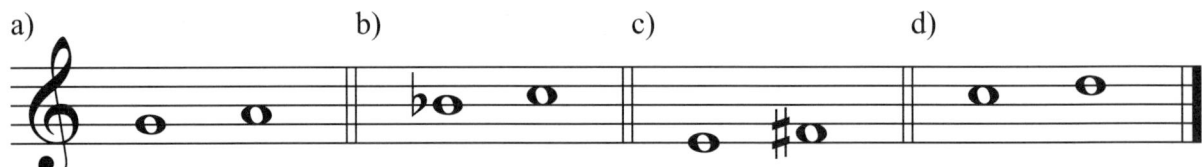

4 Melodic Dictation: Add the missing notes under the bracket. The melody will be played twice.

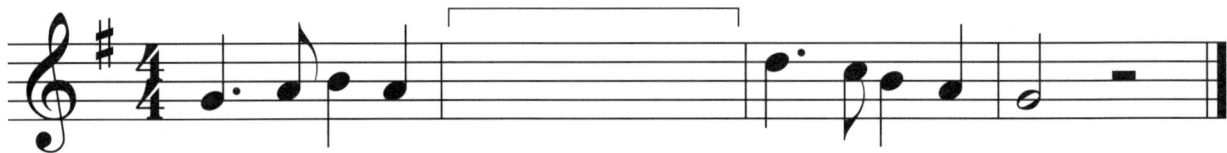

5 Rhythmic Dictation: Write the rhythmic pattern you hear in the space below. Listen as many times as you need. The rhythm is in 4/4 time.

Write it down as you hear it!

48 — Lesson 9 Ear-Training Worksheet — Sound Advice Level 3

Learning Guide — Lesson 10

A Closer Look at Writing Scales

In your Theory Worksheets, you will be asked to write scales in different ways. Read the directions carefully and remember these points:

- Make sure your scale moves in the correct direction: ascending only, descending only, or both ascending and descending.
- When you write a scale ascending and descending, you do not need to repeat the top note.
- Use whole notes unless the question specifies a different note value.
- Use a key signature when asked. If you use accidentals, check each one carefully.
- Put a double bar line at the end of the scale.

Writing Scales with Key Signatures

When you write a scale with a key signature, you do not need to add accidentals in front of the notes.

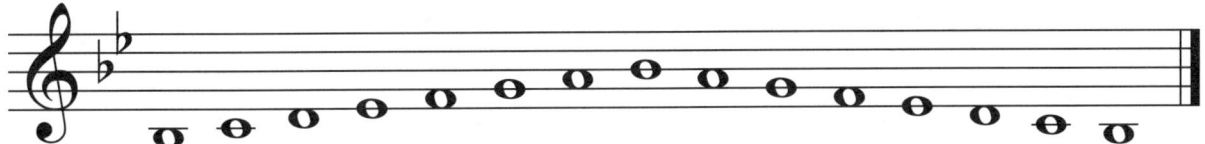

Writing Scales with Accidentals

Remember these points when you write a scale using accidentals instead of a key signature:

- Place each accidental *in front* of the note, on the same space or line as the notehead.
- Write the letter names of the sharps or flats of the key signature above the staff. Cross them out as you write the accidentals in front of the notes.
- When in doubt, double-check the pattern of whole steps and half steps.
- You do not need to repeat the accidentals for the descending half of the scale unless there is a bar line at the top.

Here are two examples:

Sound Advice Level 3   Lesson 10 Learning Guide   49

LESSON 10 Learning Guide

Chromatic Notes

The word **chromatic** comes from the Greek word *chromos*, which mean "color." A chromatic note is a note that does not belong to the key in which the music is written. Composers use chromatic notes to make a melody sound more interesting.

The following melody is in B♭ major. The notes with accidentals are chromatic notes.

To learn the sound of chromatic notes, follow these two steps:

1) Sing the first five notes of the C major scale up and down.

2) Sing these notes again, but this time, fill in the whole steps with chromatic notes between, as shown below. Each interval you sing will be a half step.

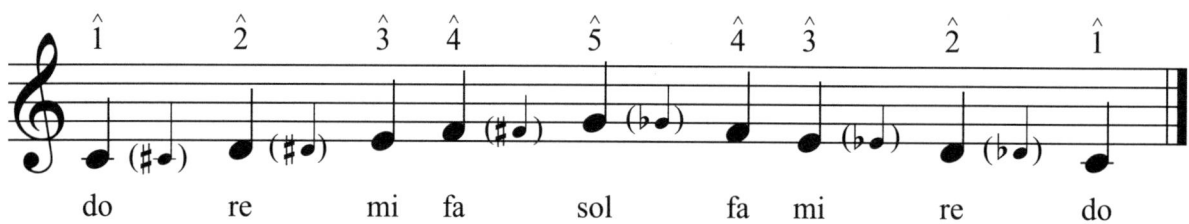

In a major scale, there is no chromatic note between 3̂ and 4̂ (mi and fa) because the distance between these two scale degrees is a half step.

You can sing this exercise using pitch syllables for the chromatic notes. (See p. 150 for information on syllable systems.)

Theory Worksheet

LESSON 10

1 Write the G major scale, ascending and descending, using accidentals.

2 Write the D major scale, descending only, using a key signature.

3 Write the B♭ major scale, ascending and descending, using accidentals.

4 Complete the following chart by filling in each blank with *one* note.

3	quarter notes	=	
8	sixteenth notes	=	
2	eighth notes	=	
2	half notes	=	
4	eighth notes	=	

5 Circle the chromatic notes in the following melody.

6 Mad Music Scores ☐ ☐ ☐

Sound Advice Level 3   Lesson 10 Theory Worksheet   51

LESSON 10 Ear-Training Worksheet

 1 **Interval Identification:** Identify the intervals you hear as min 2, maj 2, maj 3, P4, or P5.

    a)   b)   c)   d)   e)   f)   g)

 2 **Sight Singing:**
  a) Pause the recording. Sing up and down by half steps from C to G.
  b) Turn to the answer key and sing along with the recording.

3 **Error Detection:** Circle any notes that are not played correctly in the following major scale. The scale will be played twice.

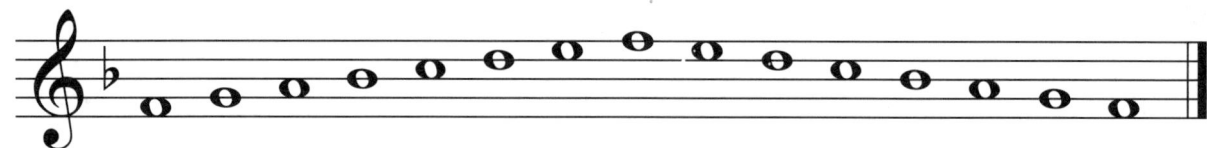

4 **Melodic Dictation:** Add the missing notes under the bracket.

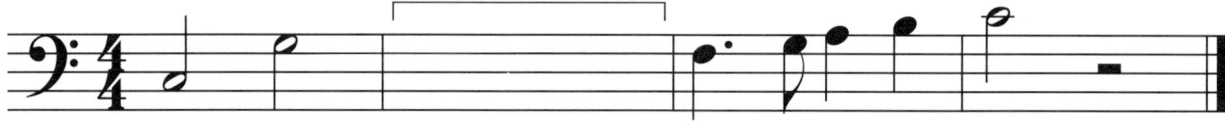

5 **Melody Singback/Playback:** Sing the melody you hear from memory, then play it back on your instrument. The melody is in B♭ major, in 2/4 time.

Learning Guide

Lesson 11

Major and Minor 3rds: A Shortcut

You have learned to identify a major 3rd by relating it to the major scale. In Example 1, the distance from F to A is a 3rd. This interval is a major 3rd because A (the upper note) belongs to the major scale that starts on F (the lower note).

The interval in Example 2 is also a 3rd. However, A♭ does not belong to the scale of F major. A♭ is a half step lower than the third note of the F major scale. Therefore, this interval is a minor 3rd.

Ex. 1

maj 3

Ex. 2

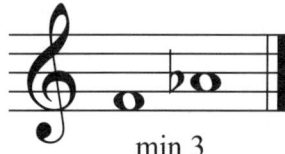

min 3

Use the following shortcut to identify whether a 3rd is major or minor:

- Major 3rds are made up of two whole steps (W+W).

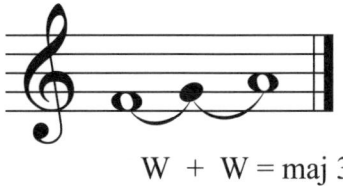
W + W = maj 3

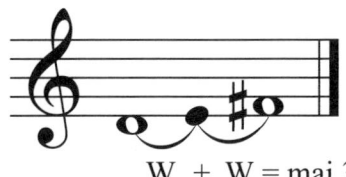
W + W = maj 3

W + W = maj 3

- Minor 3rds are made up of a whole step and a half step (W + ½) or (½ + W).

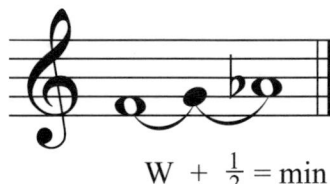
W + ½ = min

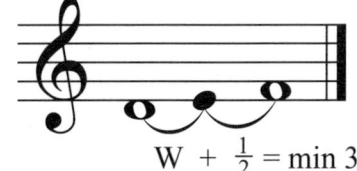
W + ½ = min 3

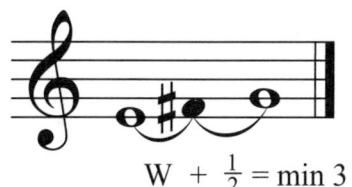
W + ½ = min 3

Sound Advice Level 3   Lesson 11 Learning Guide

LESSON 11 Learning Guide

The Sound of the Minor 3rd

Sing and play these major and minor 3rds. Compare the way they sound.

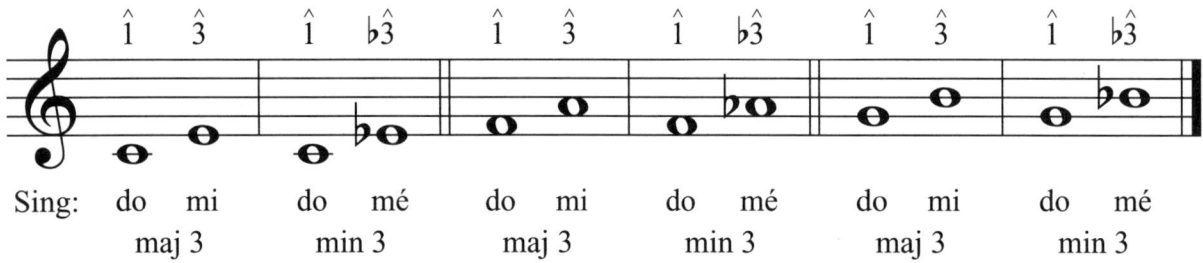

Sing:	do mi	do mé	do mi	do mé	do mi	do mé
	maj 3	min 3	maj 3	min 3	maj 3	min 3

Turn to the Song Clue Chart on p. 119 and put a ✔ beside the minor 3rd (min 3).

Measure Numbers

When you learn a piece of music, its always a good idea to number the measures. The *first complete* measure is measure 1 (m. 1).

When you number the measures in your own music, write the number above the first beat of each measure.

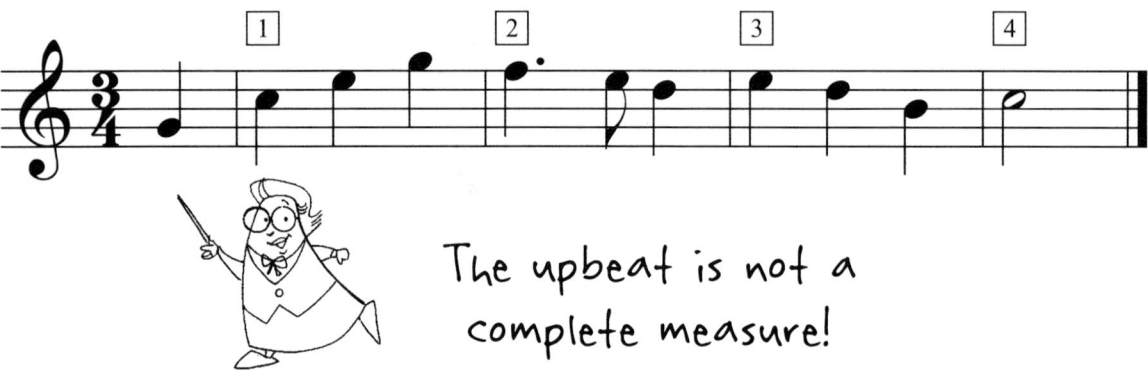

The upbeat is not a complete measure!

Theory Worksheet — Lesson 11

1 Turn each major 3rd into a minor 3rd by rewriting the given notes and writing the appropriate accidental in front of the upper note.

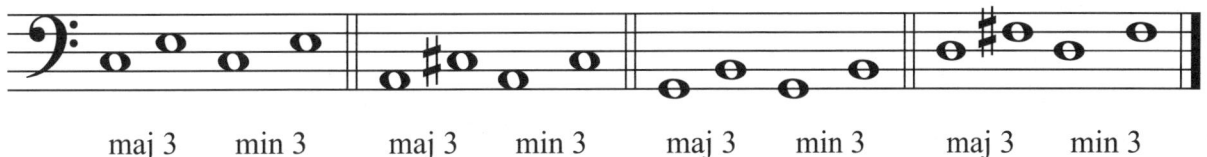

maj 3   min 3   maj 3   min 3   maj 3   min 3   maj 3   min 3

2 a) Identify the order of steps by circling W + W or W + $\frac{1}{2}$ above the following intervals.

b) Name the intervals as major 3rds or minor 3rds. The first one has been done for you.

min 3   _____   _____   _____   _____

3 Circle the quarter-note beats, then add measure numbers and the correct time signature.

Hornpipe
Z 685

Henry Purcell
(1659–1695)

4 Replace the dots on the following notes with a tied note that has the same value. The first one has been done for you.

𝅝. = 𝅝 ⌒ 𝅗𝅥   𝅗𝅥. = _____

𝅗𝅥. = _____   ♪. = _____

5 Mad Music Scores ☐ ☐ ☐

LESSON 11 Ear-Training Worksheet

1 Sight Singing:
   a) Pause the recording. Sing the following melody while you tap a steady quarter-note beat.
   b) Turn to the answer key and sing along with the recording.

2 Interval Identification: Identify the intervals you hear as min 2, maj 2, min 3, or maj 3.

a)   b)   c)   d)   e)   f)   g)

3 Editing: The following intervals are written as major 3rds. If you hear a major 3rd, leave the interval as written. If you hear a minor 3rd, write the appropriate accidental in front of the upper note.

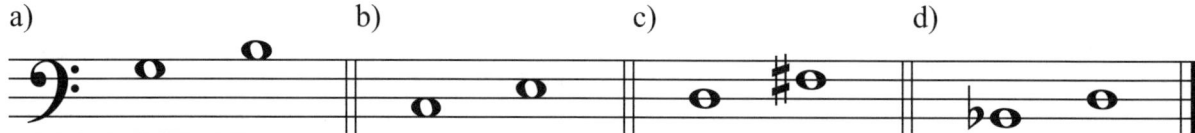

4 Melodic Dictation: Add the missing notes under the bracket.

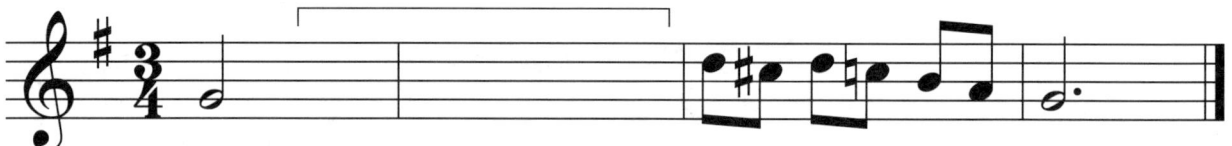

5 Rhythmic Dictation: Write the rhythmic pattern you hear in the space below. The rhythm is in $\frac{2}{4}$ time.

Learning Guide — Lesson 12

Major Triads

A **chord** consists of three or more pitches that sound together.
A **triad** is a chord that has three notes.

A **major triad** consists of the first, third, and fifth notes of a major scale ($\hat{1}$–$\hat{3}$–$\hat{5}$).

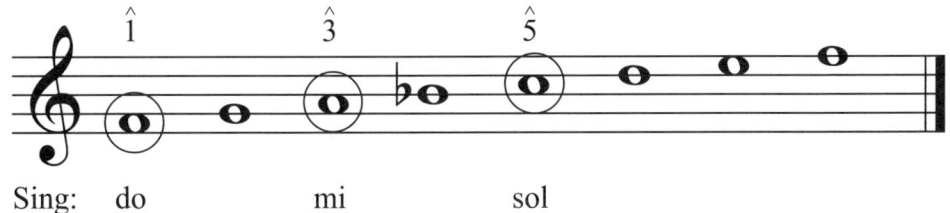

Sing: do   mi   sol

The notes of a triad can be played **solid** (blocked) or **broken** (one after the other).

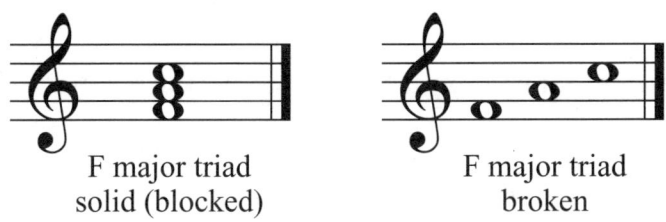

F major triad solid (blocked)   F major triad broken

The bottom note of a triad is called the **root**. The middle note is called the **third**. The top note is called the **fifth**. Triads are always identified by their roots.

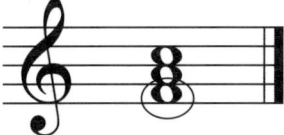 

F major triad: root = F   D major triad: root = D

A Stack of 3rds

The interval between the root and the middle note of a triad is a 3rd. The interval between the root and the top note is a 5th. You can also see that a major triad is made up of two 3rds stacked one on top of the other.

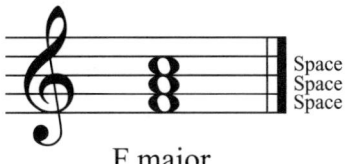 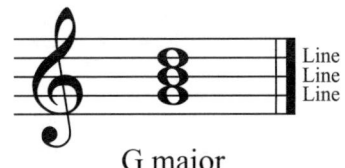

F major   G major

Triads look like snowmen!

LESSON 12 Learning Guide

The bottom 3rd is a major 3rd (W + W).
The top 3rd is a minor 3rd (W + $\frac{1}{2}$).

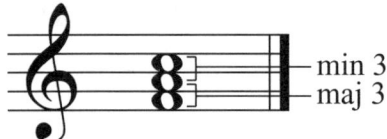 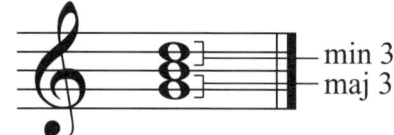

A Closer Look at the Minor 3rd

You have learned to write a minor 3rd by lowering the upper note of a major 3rd.

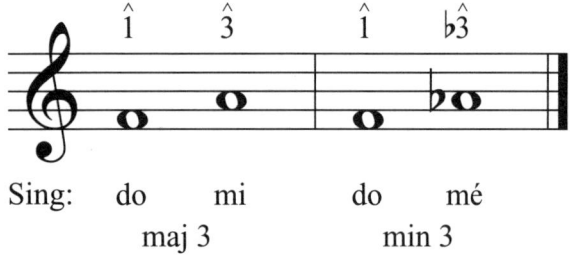

Sing: do   mi   do   mé
      maj 3   min 3

Most familiar melodies that begin with an ascending minor 3rd actually begin on the *third* note of a major scale ($\hat{3}$).

Sing this broken major triad. The distance from $\hat{3}$ up to $\hat{5}$ (mi to sol) is an ascending minor 3rd. The distance from $\hat{5}$ down to $\hat{3}$ (sol to mi) is a descending minor 3rd.

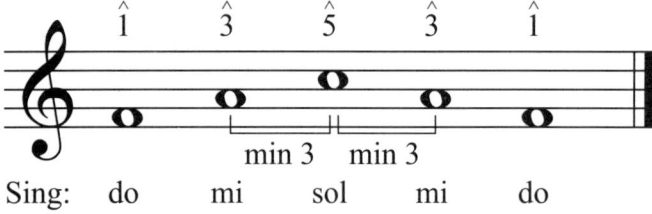

Sing: do   mi   sol   mi   do

Rhythm Jumble Games

On your Theory Worksheets, you have been recording the number of times you used the Rhythm Jumble Chart to practice sight reading rhythms. From now on you can play one of these Rhythm Jumble Games:

Rhythm Jumble Reading
Rhythm Jumble Solitaire
Rhythm Jumble Composer

Play one of these games at least three times before your next lesson. Write your scores in the boxes on your Theory Worksheets. Ask your teacher which one you should start with.

Theory Worksheet — Lesson 12

1 a) Write the G major scale, ascending only, in whole notes. Use a key signature.

b) Circle the notes that make a G major triad.

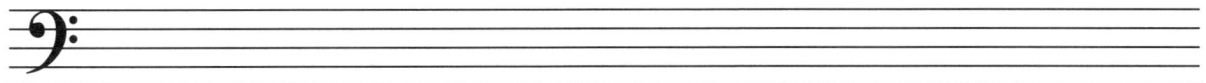

2 a) Write the following triads on the staff, using accidentals.

b) Draw these triads on the keyboard, using curved lines. Label the 3rds as major or minor. The first one has been done for you.

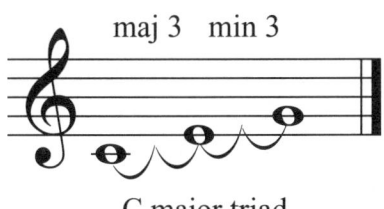

C major triad

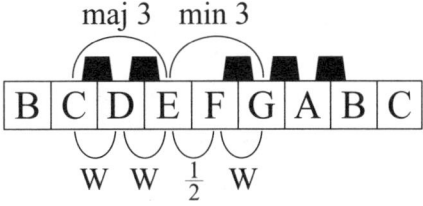

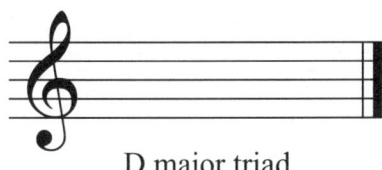

D major triad

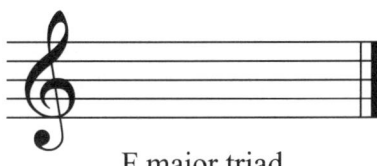

F major triad

3 Circle the quarter-note beats. Add bar lines according to the time signature.

a)

b)

4 Rhythm Jumble Scores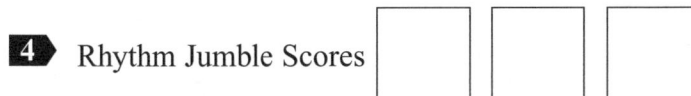

Sound Advice Level 3

LESSON 12 — Ear-Training Worksheet

1 **Interval Identification:** Identify the intervals you hear as ascending (↗) min 2, maj 2, min 3, maj 3, P4, P5, or descending (↘) min 3.

a)   b)   c)   d)   e)   f)   g)

2 **Sight Singing:**
a) Pause the recording. Sing the following melody while you tap a steady quarter-note beat.
b) Turn to the answer key and sing along with the recording.

3 **Triads:** You will hear a major triad followed by either the root or the third. Write the note you hear beside each triad. Each example will be played twice.

a)   b)   c)   d)

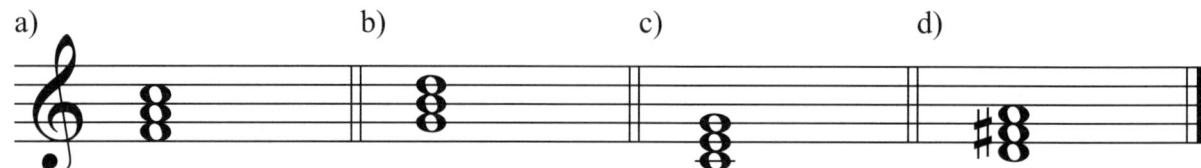

4 **Error Detection:** Circle any notes that are not played correctly in the melody below. Rewrite the melody to show how it was played on the recording. The melody will be played twice.

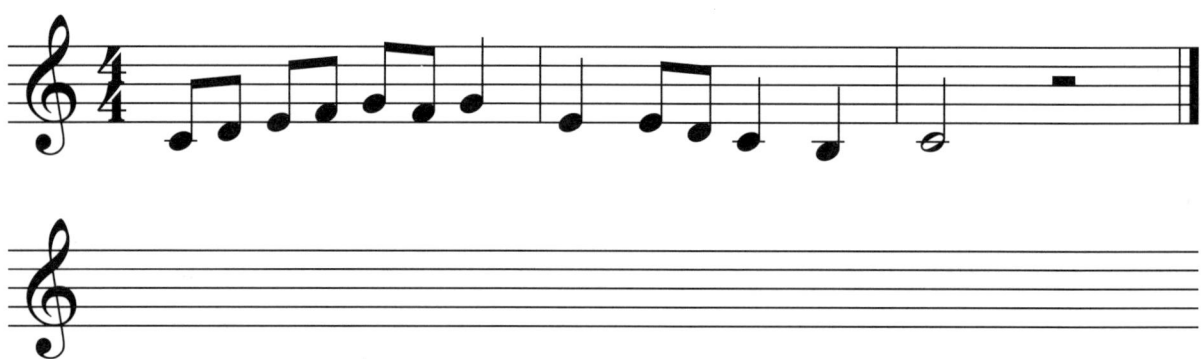

5 **Editing:** The following intervals are written as major 3rds. If you hear a major 3rd, leave the interval as written. If you hear a minor 3rd, write the appropriate accidental in front of the *upper* note.

a)   b)   c)   d)   e)

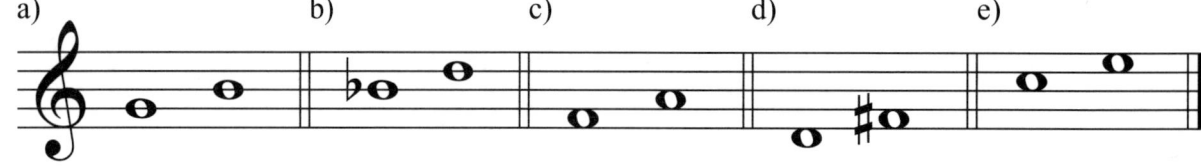

Phrases

A **phrase** is like a musical sentence. The notes in a phrase sound as if they belong together. Many phrases end with a long note. Most melodies are made up of two or more phrases. Phrases are sometimes marked with a slur.

Cadences

All phrases end with a **cadence**. A cadence is like a punctuation mark in a sentence. Some cadences sound like endings, or periods. Others sound like pauses, or commas. For example, if you read a long sentence that has a comma part way through, you pause, but then continue. When you come to the period at the end of the sentence, you stop.

A melodic cadence usually involves the last two notes of the phrase. In most melodies, the last note of the phrase is longer than the others.

Play or sing the following melody. Compare the two cadences marked with brackets. Which one sounds more final?

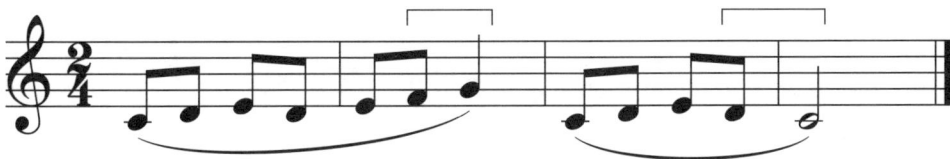

Melodic Imitation

The word "imitate" means "to copy." Composers frequently use imitation when they create melodies. Play or sing these two melodies, and listen to the phrases.

- The phrases are marked with slurs.
- The melodies are made up of two short phrases.
- The second phrase starts out exactly like the first. In other words, m. 3 imitates m. 1.
- The fourth measure is different from the second measure. It has been changed so that the melody ends on the tonic.

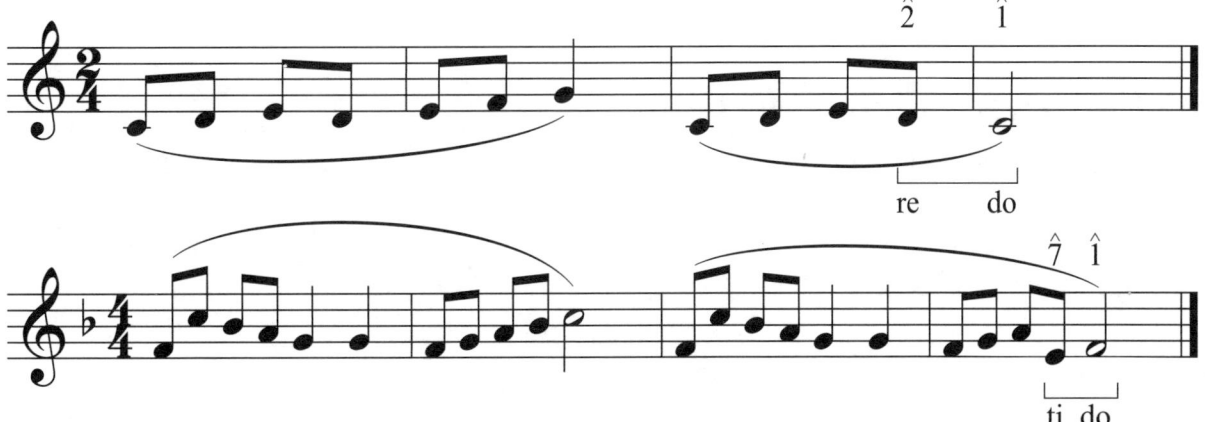

Now look at the endings of the two melodies.

- Both melodies end on the tonic, and the tonic is approached by step.
- In the first melody, the tonic—C—is approached by a step from above: $\hat{2}$ down to $\hat{1}$ (re–do).
- In the second melody, tonic—F—is approached by a step from below: $\hat{7}$ up to $\hat{1}$ (ti–do).

LESSON 13 Learning Guide

Composing and Improvising

In Level 2, you learned how to create a melody by **composing** a response to a two-measure opening. You often used imitation in your melodies. Sometimes you were asked to write your melodic response. Other times, you were asked to make it up on the spot, which is called **improvising**. You will do more melodic improvisation beginning with this lesson.

The Sound of the Descending Major 2nd

In a descending major scale, all the scale degrees are a major 2nd apart except for $\hat{1}$ down to $\hat{7}$ (do down to ti) and $\hat{4}$ down to $\hat{3}$ (fa down to mi). Many melodies begin with a descending major 2nd from $\hat{3}$ down to $\hat{2}$ (mi down to re) and $\hat{2}$ down to $\hat{1}$ (re down to do). Play or sing these two familiar songs.

Both tunes begin with a three-note descending pattern. You will often find this same three-note descending pattern at the cadence point that ends a phrase. Play or sing the following melody, and listen to the descending major 2nds, especially at the cadence point:

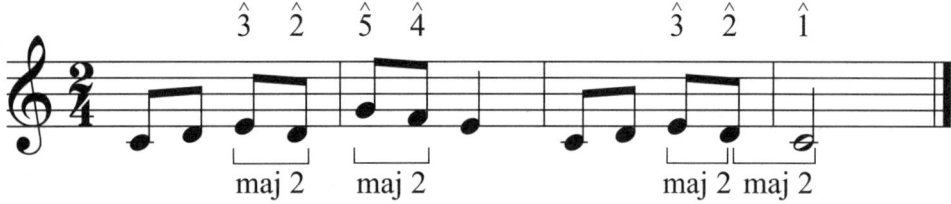

The Sound of the Descending Perfect 4th

You can often hear a descending perfect 4th (P4) in melodies between $\hat{1}$ and $\hat{5}$ (do down to sol). Play or sing the following melody.

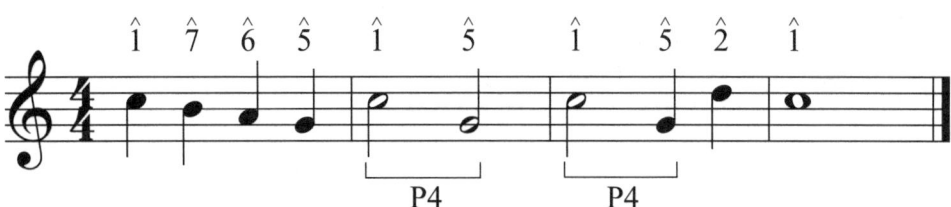

Turn to the Song Clue Chart on p. 119 and put a ✔ beside the descending major 2nd (maj 2) and the descending perfect 4th (P4).

Theory Worksheet — LESSON 13

1 Draw a line to connect each group of notes on the left with its corresponding note value on the right.

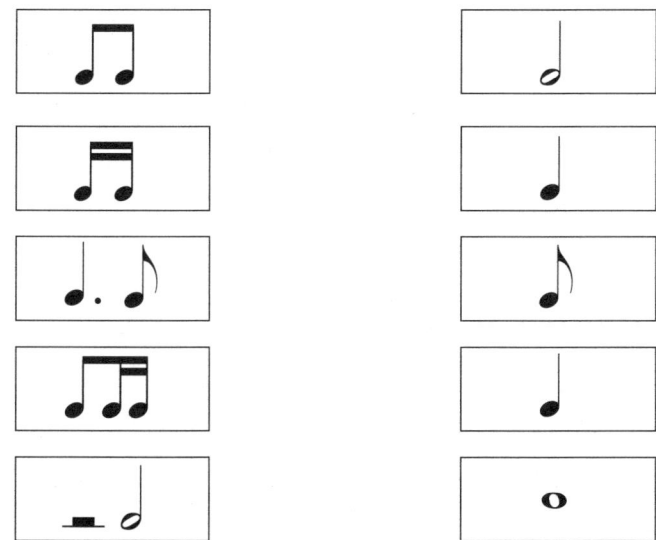

2 Play or sing the following melody, then answer the questions below.

a) Name the key. _____

b) Write the measure numbers on the score.

c) How many measures does this melody have? _____

d) Does this melody sound finished? _____

e) Which measure contains the lowest note? _____

f) Draw brackets to mark the imitation.

3 a) Sing or play the following two-measure melodic opening, then improvise a response. Your response should imitate the first measure and end on the tonic.

b) Write your response on the staff.

4 Name the following intervals. Remember to think of the major key and scale of the lower note.

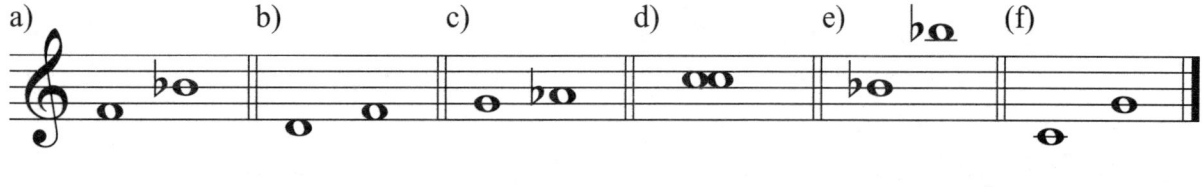

5 Mad Music Scores ☐ ☐ ☐

Sound Advice Level 3 Lesson 13 Theory Worksheet 63

LESSON 13: Ear-Training Worksheet

1. Interval Identification: Identify the intervals you hear as ascending (↗) min 2, maj 2, min 3, maj 3, P4, P5, descending (↘) maj 2, min 3, or P4.

a)   b)   c)   d)   e)

f)   g)   h)   i)   j)

2. Sight Singing:
 a) Pause the recording. Sing up and down by half steps from C to G.
 b) Turn to the answer key and sing along with the recording.

3. Rhythmic Dictation:
 a) Clap the *rhythm* of the melody you hear from memory.
 b) Write it in the space below. The melody is in 3/4 time.

4. Melodic Dictation:
 a) Sing the melody you hear from memory.
 b) Write it on the staff below. The melody is in F major, in 2/4 time.

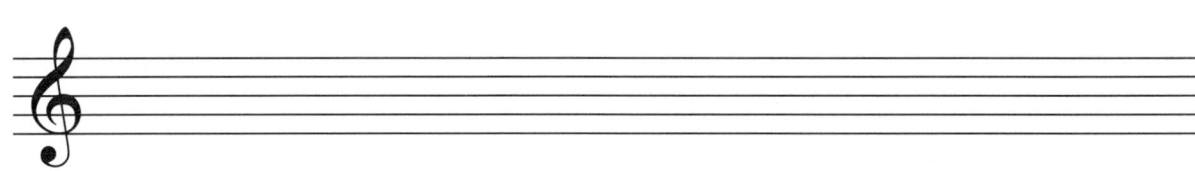

Your answer should follow in strict time—don't hesitate.

5. Melodic Improvisation: You will hear a two-measure opening.
 a) Improvise a two-measure response.
 b) Write your response on the staff below. Your melody should end on the tonic.

Opening: Response:

Minor Triads

A major triad is made up of two 3rds—a minor 3rd on top of a major 3rd. If you lower the middle note of a major triad by a half step, two things happen:

- The triad becomes a minor triad.
- The quality of the two 3rds that make up the triad changes. Now the minor 3rd is on the bottom.

Compare the major and minor triads below.

F major triad

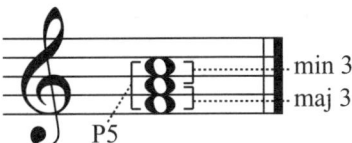
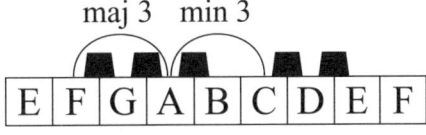

F minor triad

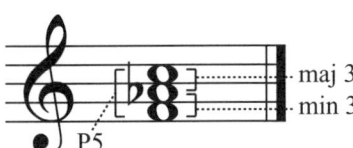
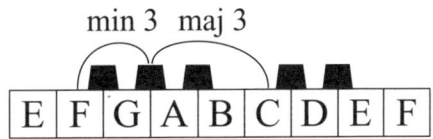

To change a triad from major to minor, you need to lower the middle note (the third of the triad).

- If the third of the major triad has no accidental, you will need a flat sign.
- If the third has a sharp, you will need a natural sign.

Play the following pairs of triads and listen to the contrast in sound. Notice the accidentals on the minor triads.

Sing the following exercise to memorize the sound of major and minor triads:

Sound Advice Level 3

LESSON 14 Learning Guide

Points to remember for major and minor triads:

- Major triads are made up of a major 3rd on the bottom and a minor 3rd on the top.
- Minor triads are made up of a minor 3rd on the bottom and a major 3rd on the top.
- In both major and minor triads, the two outer notes—the root and the fifth—are a perfect 5th apart.

The Sound of the Descending Perfect 5th

Sing this exercise that combines the sound of major and minor triads and the descending perfect 5th.

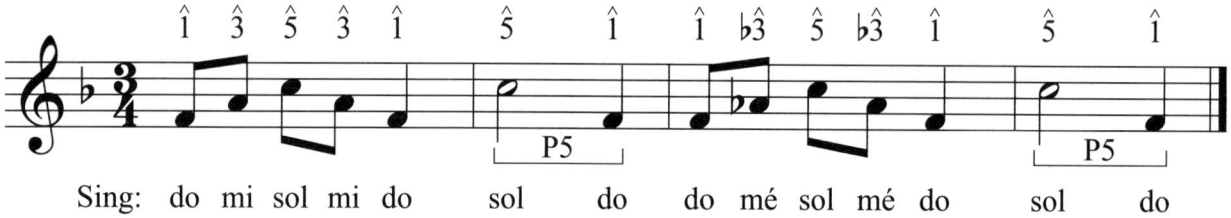

Sing: do mi sol mi do   sol   do   do mé sol mé do   sol   do

Turn to the Song Clue Chart on p. 119 and put a ✔ beside the descending perfect 5th.

Theory Worksheet — Lesson 14

1 Turn the following major triads into minor triads by adding accidentals.

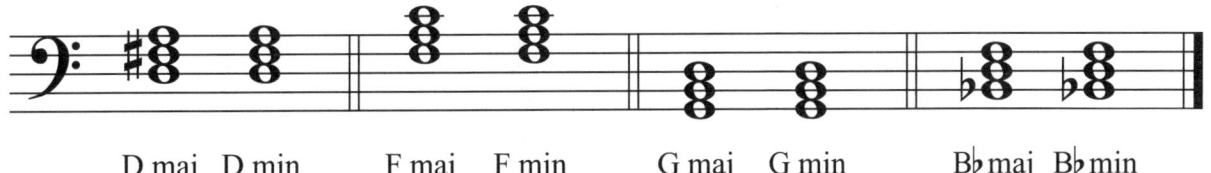

D maj   D min   F maj   F min   G maj   G min   B♭ maj   B♭ min

2 Draw curved arrows on the keyboards below to show the following major and minor triads.

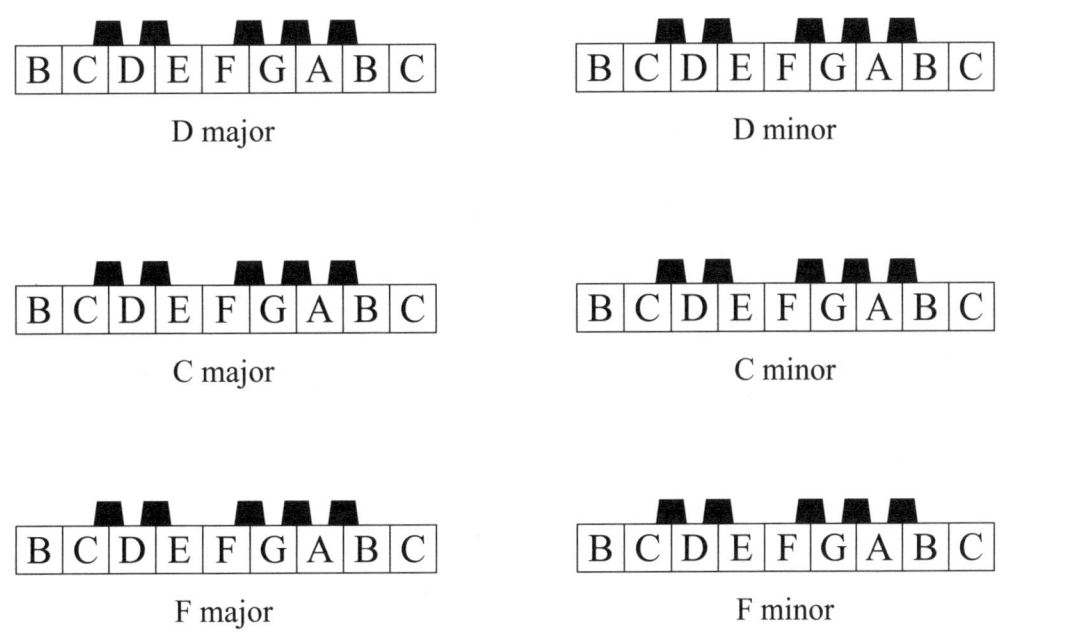

3 Circle the quarter-note beats, then add the time signature to each of the following rhythms.

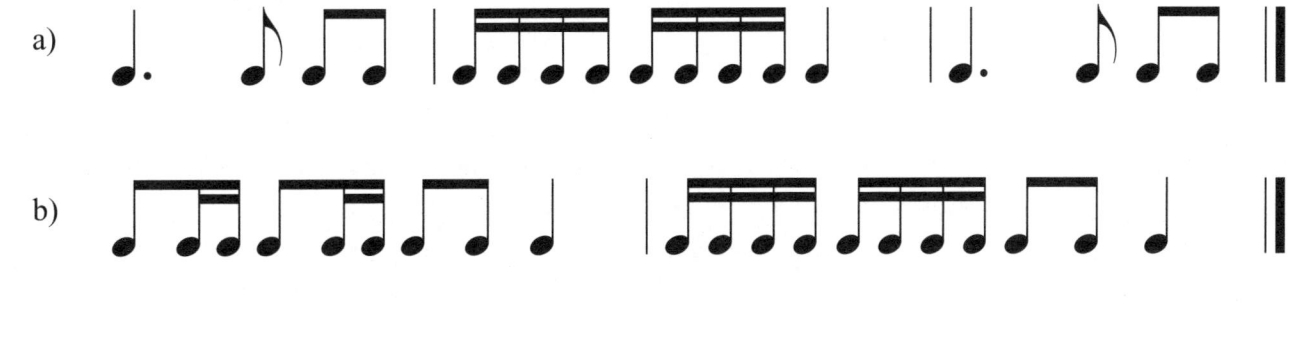

4 Rhythm Jumble Scores ☐ ☐ ☐

LESSON 14
Ear-Training Worksheet

 1 **Interval Identification:** Identify the intervals you hear as ↗ min 2, maj 2, min 3, maj 3, P4, P5, ↘ maj 2, min 3, P4, or P5.

a)   b)   c)   d)   e)

f)   g)   h)   i)   j)

 2 **Triad Identification:** Identify the triads you hear as major or minor. Each triad will be played twice.

a)   b)   c)   d)   e)

 3 **Sight Singing:**
  a) Pause the recording. Sing the following melody while you tap a steady quarter-note beat.
  b) Turn to the answer key and sing along with the recording.

 4 **Rhythmic Dictation:**
  a) Clap the *rhythm* of the melody you hear from memory.
  b) Write it in the space below. The rhythm is in 3/4 time.

 5 **Error Detection:** Compare the melody you hear with the melody written below, and circle any differences. Rewrite the melody as it was played on the recording.

Minuet in G
BWV Anh. 114

Christian Petzold
(1677–1733)

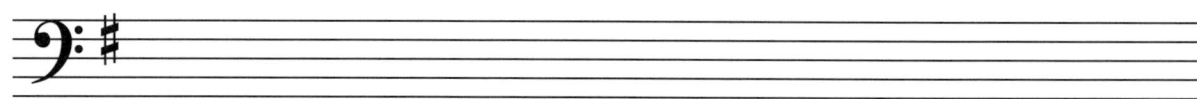

Learning Guide — Lesson 15

A Closer Look at Rests

As you know, any note can be replaced by a rest of the same length:

$$\mathbf{o} = \rule{0.5em}{0.4em}$$

$$\mathbf{d} = \rule{0.5em}{0.4em}$$

$$\mathbf{\downarrow} = \mathbf{\}}$$

$$\mathbf{\eighthnote} = \mathbf{\gamma}$$ These are new!

$$\mathbf{\sixteenthnote} = \mathbf{\gamma}$$

When you write rests on a staff, make sure you put them in the correct place as shown in the example below. Pay special attention to half rests and whole rests. The placement is the same for the treble and bass staff

 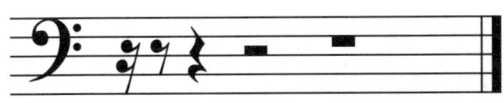

New Rhythmic Unit

Sing the following rhythms while you tap a steady quarter-note beat. On the rests, you can be silent or say "sh."

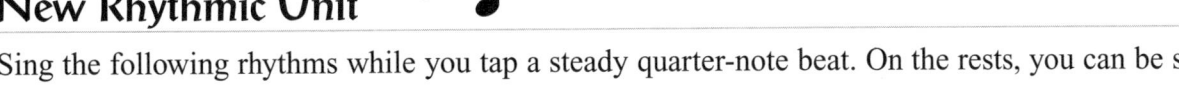

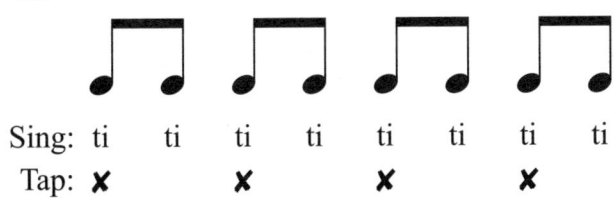

Sing: ti ti ti ti ti ti ti ti
Tap: ✗   ✗   ✗   ✗

Sing: ti   ti   ti   ti
Tap: ✗   ✗   ✗   ✗

Sound Advice Level 3

Lesson 15 Learning Guide

A Closer Look at Note Values

Here is another way to remember how note values relate to each other. Look at the notes in Example 1 below.

Begin at "Start here," and read the notes as you follow the arrows upward. Each pair of notes in a shaded area is equal in length to the single note directly above it.

Example 1

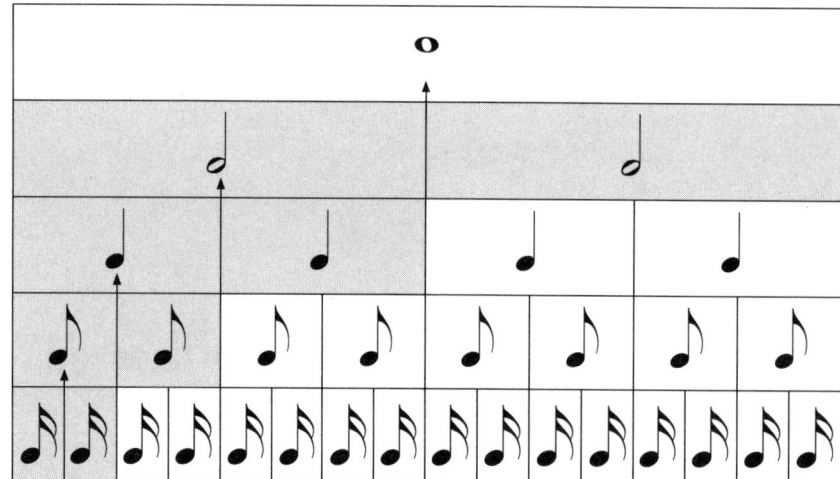

Now follow the notes and arrows in Example 2 below. This method is called "Move Up by Matching."

Example 2

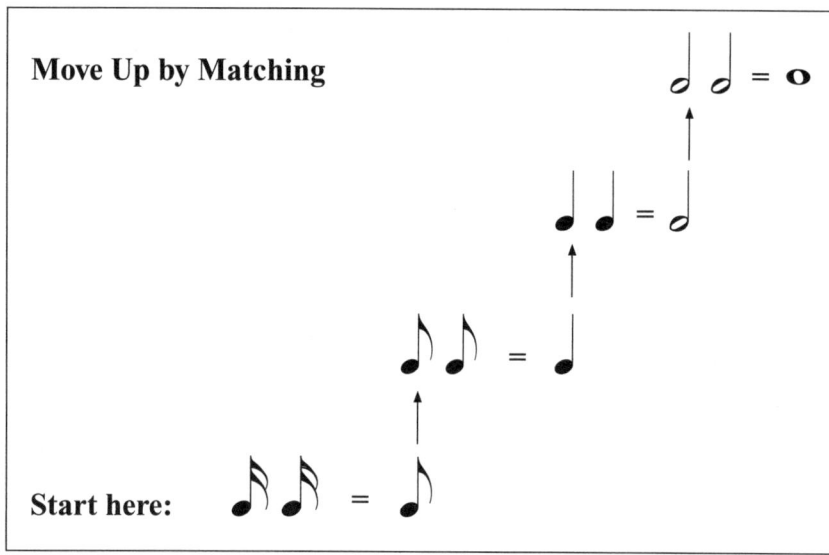

Theory Worksheet — Lesson 15

1 Draw a line to connect each group on the left with its corresponding note value on the right.

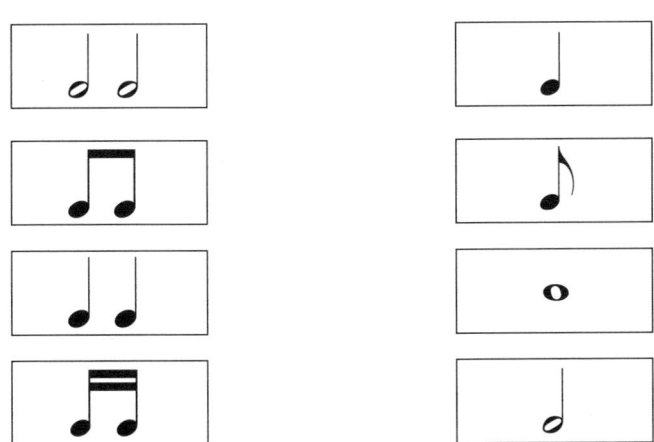

2 Draw a line to connect each group on the left with its corresponding note value on the right.

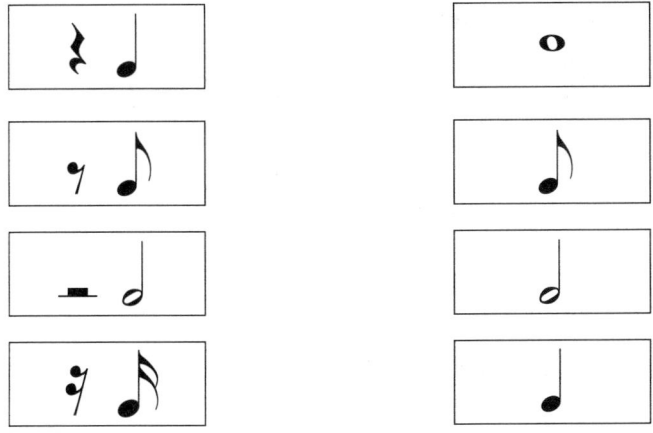

3 Circle the quarter-note beats. Add bar lines according to the time signature.

4 Practice drawing the rests on the Drawing Symbols Chart (p. 114).

5 Rhythm Jumble Scores ☐ ☐ ☐

LESSON 15: Ear-Training Worksheet

 1 **Interval Identification:** Identify the intervals you hear as ↗ min 2, maj 2, min 3, maj 3, P4, P5, ↘ maj 2, min 3, P4, or P5.

a)   b)   c)   d)   e)

f)   g)   h)   i)   j)

 2 **Triad Identification:** Identify the triads you hear as major or minor.

a)   b)   c)   d)   e)

 3 **Triads:** You will hear a minor triad followed by either its root or its third. Write the note that you hear on the staff beside each triad.

a)   b)   c)   d)

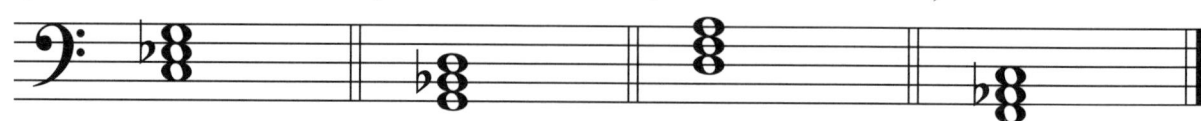

 4 **Rhythmic Reading:**
a) Pause the recording. Sing the following rhythmic pattern while you tap a steady quarter-note beat.

b) Turn to the answer key and sing along with the recording.

 5 **Rhythmic Identification:** Identify the correct notation for the rhythmic pattern you hear.

Ear-Training Worksheet
LESSON 15

 6 **Rhythmic Dictation:** Add the missing notes under the bracket. The pattern will be played twice.

 7 **Melodic Improvisation:** You will hear a two-measure opening.
a) Improvise a two-measure response.
b) Write your response on the staff below. Your melody should end on the tonic.

Don't hesitate!

Sound Advice Level 3   Lesson 15 Ear-Training Worksheet

Arpeggios

You can create a four-note chord, or **arpeggio**, by doubling the root of a triad an octave above. Sing or play the following one-octave arpeggios.

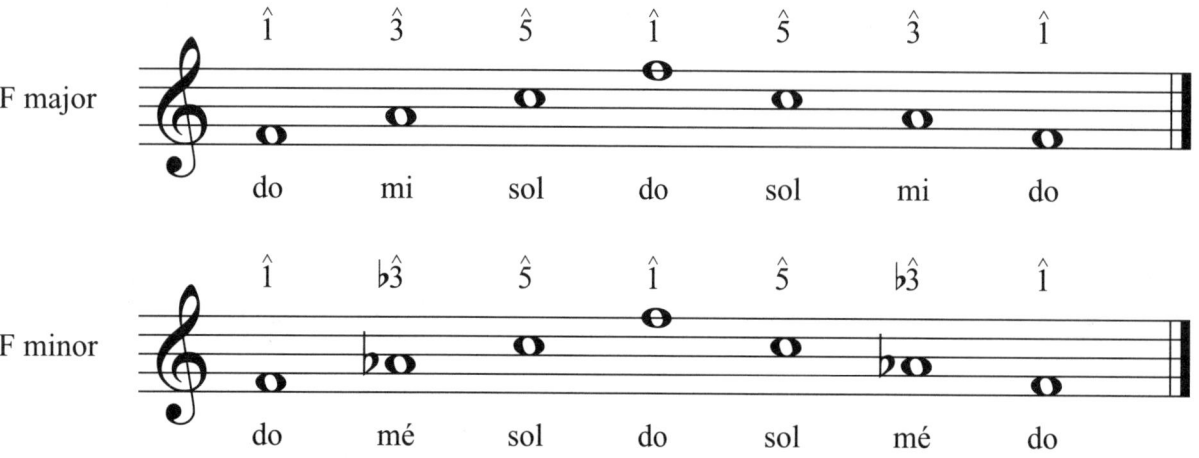

Play this two-octave C major arpeggio.

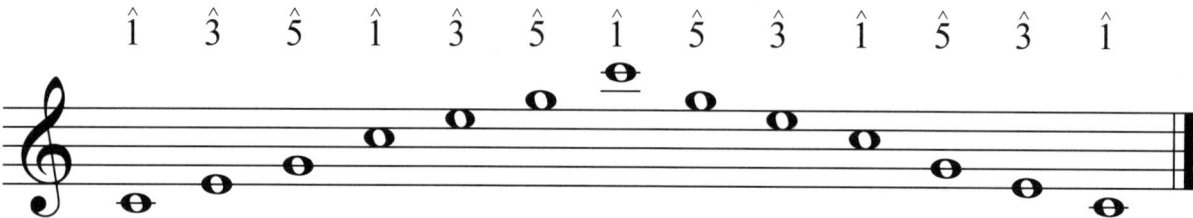

The Sound of the Perfect Octave

To memorize the sound of a perfect octave (P8), sing a one-octave major scale starting on $\hat{1}$ (do), then repeat the lowest and highest notes.

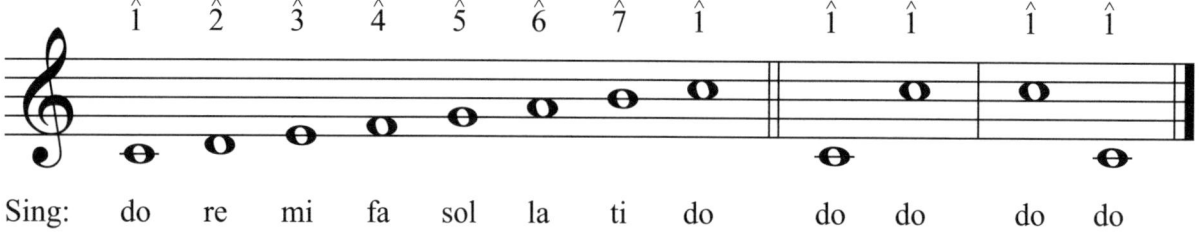

You can also sing a one-octave arpeggio, then repeat the lowest and highest notes.

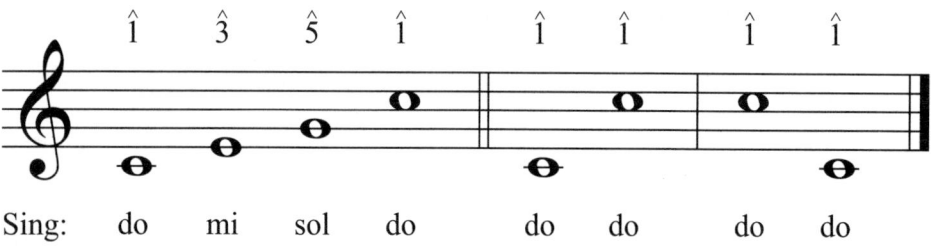

Learning Guide

LESSON 16

Turn to the Song Clue Chart on p. 119 and put a ✔ beside the ascending and descending P8.

Interval Hint:
If you find it difficult to identify an interval that you hear, follow these steps:

1) Memorize the two notes.

2) Sing the two notes in the opposite direction. Think of "flipping" the interval.

3) Try to recognize the "flipped" interval, or match it with one of your song clues.

New Rhythmic Unit

Sing the following rhythms while you tap a steady beat. On the rests, you can be silent or say "sh."

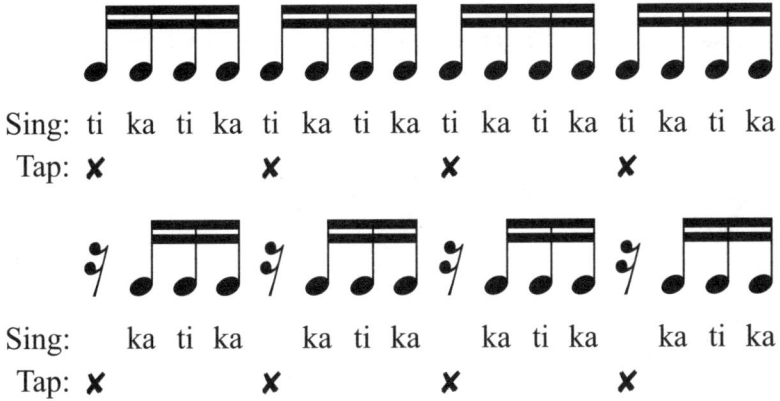

Turn to the Rhythm Jumble Chart on p. 115 and circle the unit.

Stem Direction

You have learned that the stems of notes above the middle line go down, and the stems of notes below the middle line go up. Stems of notes on the middle line can go up or down, but down is preferred.

For beamed notes, all the stems go in the same direction as the note that is the farthest away from the middle line.

Make sure your notes look like "p's" or "d's". Think of pay day!

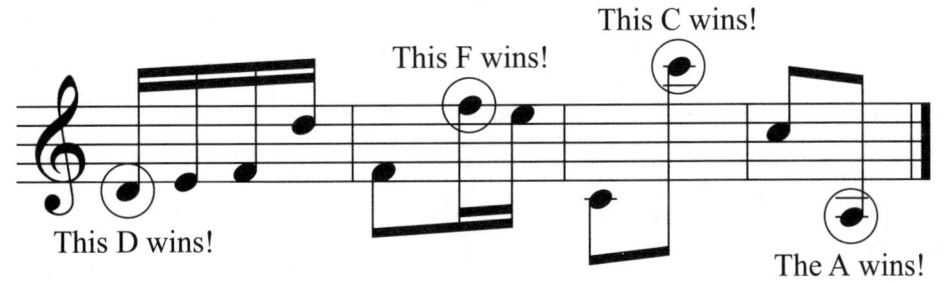

Sound Advice Level 3 — Lesson 16 Learning Guide — 75

LESSON 16 Theory Worksheet

1 Draw curved arrows on the keyboards to show the following one-octave arpeggios.

C major arpeggio   C minor arpeggio

2 Draw curved arrows on the keyboards below to show the following triads.

D major triad   D minor triad

3 Rewrite the following melody, beaming the notes to show the quarter-note beat. Pay attention to the direction of the stems. Add bar lines.

4 Draw a line to connect each group on the left with its corresponding note value on the right.

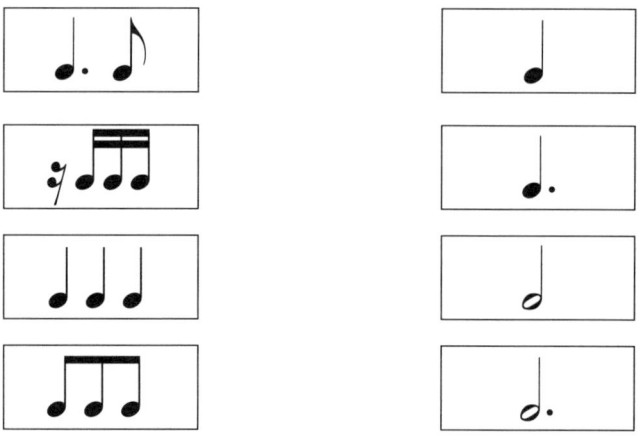

5 Circle the quarter-note beats. Add bar lines according to the time signature.

6 Mad Music Scores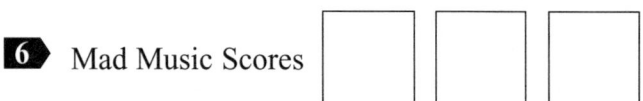

Ear-Training Worksheet

LESSON 16

 1 **Interval Identification:** Name the intervals you hear as ↗ min 2, maj 2, min 3, maj 3, P4, P5, P8, ↘ maj 2, min 3, P4, P5, or P8.

a)   b)   c)   d)   e)

f)   g)   h)   i)   j)

 2 **Rhythmic Reading:**
  a) Pause the recording. Sing the following rhythmic pattern while you tap a steady quarter-note beat.
  b) Turn to the answer key and sing along with the recording.

 3 **Rhythmic Dictation:** Add the missing notes under the bracket.

 4 **Triad Identification:** Identify the triads you hear as major or minor.

a)   b)   c)   d)   e)

 5 **Triads:** You will hear a minor triad followed by either its root or its third. Write the note that you hear on the staff beside each triad.

a)   b)   c)   d)

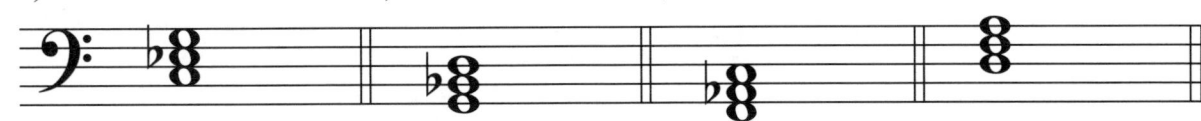

LESSON 16 Ear-Training Worksheet

 6 **Error Detection:** Compare the melody you hear with the melody written below, and circle any differences. Rewrite the melody as it was played on the recording.

Learning Guide — Lesson 17

Rhythmic Imitation

Composers frequently use **imitation** when they create melodies. Imitation can be melodic, rhythmic, or both melodic and rhythmic.

Sing the following rhythmic patterns while you tap a steady beat.

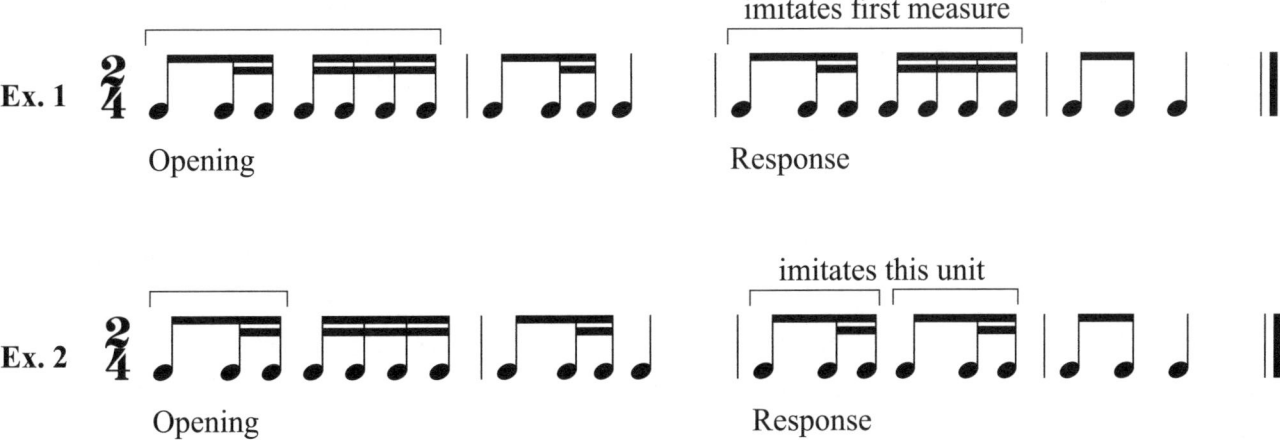

Examples 1 and 2 each consist of an opening and a response.

- The responses sound unified because they imitate the opening.
- The long notes at the end provide a resting point or cadence.

Sing Example 3 below while you tap a steady beat. Compare it to the two examples above.

You probably agree that Example 3 is not as good as Examples 1 and 2.

- Example 3 does not use imitation.
- The final eighth note does not provide a resting point or cadence.

In the Theory Worksheet for this lesson, you will be asked to improvise a two-measure response to a given two-measure rhythmic opening. Make sure you include some type of imitation in at least one measure of the response. End your response with a note that will bring the phrase to a close. Try out several different responses. When you have created one you are happy with, write it down.

LESSON 17 Theory Worksheet

1 Sing the following rhythmic patterns, then draw a bracket over any examples of imitation.

a)

b)

2 Sing the following examples, then indicate whether you feel a cadence at the end.

a) ❏ cadence ❏ no cadence

b) ❏ cadence ❏ no cadence

3 Sing the following examples, then indicate whether the last two measures make a good or a poor response.

a)  ❏ good ❏ poor

b)  ❏ good ❏ poor

c)  ❏ good ❏ poor

4 a) Sing the following rhythmic opening, then improvise a two-measure response.

b) When you are happy with your response, write it in the space below.

Ear-Training Worksheet

LESSON 17

 1 **Interval Identification:** The first note of each interval is given. Name the interval and write the second note. Each interval will be played twice.

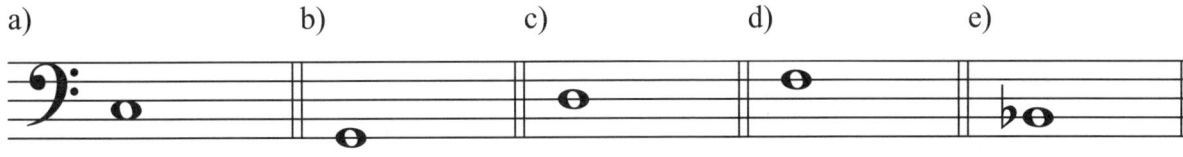

 2 **Rhythmic Dictation:**
a) Clap the *rhythm* of the melody you hear from memory.
b) Write it in the space below. The melody is in $\frac{4}{4}$ time.

 3 **Melodic Dictation:** Add the missing notes under the bracket. The melody will be played twice.

 4 **Rhythmic Improvisation:** You will hear a two-measure opening.
a) Improvise a two-measure rhythmic response.
b) Write your response in the space below.

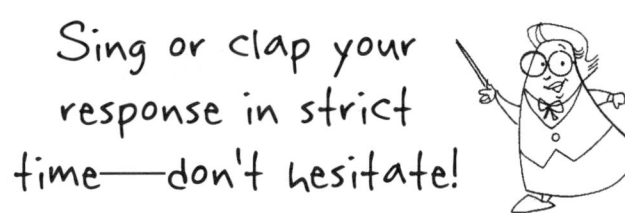

 5 **Melodic Improvisation:** You will hear a two-measure opening.
a) Improvise a two-measure response.
b) Write your response on the staff below. Your melody should end on the tonic.

Opening: Response:

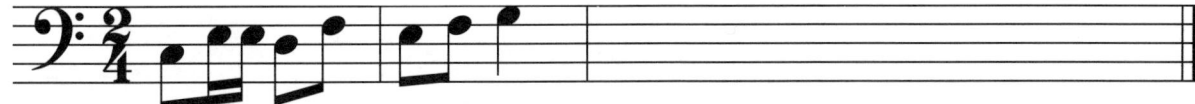

Learning Guide

Melodic Imitation

As we have learned, imitation is an important element in music. Most composers use some form of imitation in their melodies.

You have been improvising two-measure responses by imitating the first measure, then changing the second measure to end on the tonic, as shown in Example 1.

A Tune

Ex. 1   Anon.

The excerpts below are from the *Notebook for Anna Magdalena Bach*, compiled by Johann Sebastian Bach. Play or sing these examples to see how the composer used imitation.

In Example 2, the second measure imitates the first measure exactly, but the third and fourth measures are different.

Musette in D Major
BWV Anh. 126

Ex. 2   Anon.

In Example 3, the second measure imitates the first measure, but one step lower. The third and fourth measures are different. The dotted half note creates a strong feeling of cadence at the end.

Minuet in G Major
BWV Anh. 116

Ex. 3   Anon.

Look for different types of imitation in the music you are playing.

Learning Guide

LESSON 18

The Sound of the Major 6th

Play and sing this example. In m. 3, the interval from $\hat{5}$ up to $\hat{3}$ (sol to mi) is a major 6th.

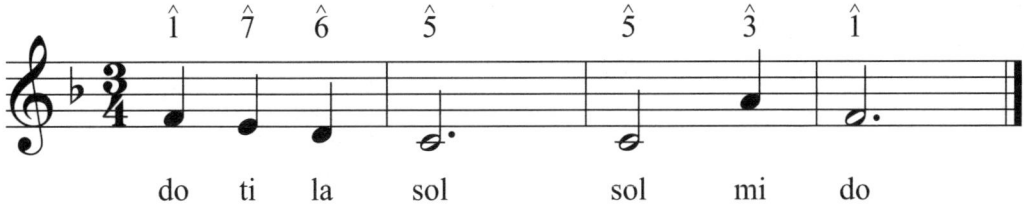

Song Clues for the Major 6th

The following melodies begin with a major 6th from $\hat{5}$ up to $\hat{3}$ (sol to mi). Play or sing each one.

Turn to the Song Clue Chart on p. 119 and put a ✔ beside the major 6th.

Sound Advice Level 3   Lesson 18 Learning Guide   83

LESSON 18 Theory Worksheet

1 Sing or play the following melodies, then draw a bracket over any examples of imitation.

a)

b)

2 a) Sing or play this two-measure melodic opening, then improvise a response.

b) Write your response on the staff. Your response should end on the tonic.

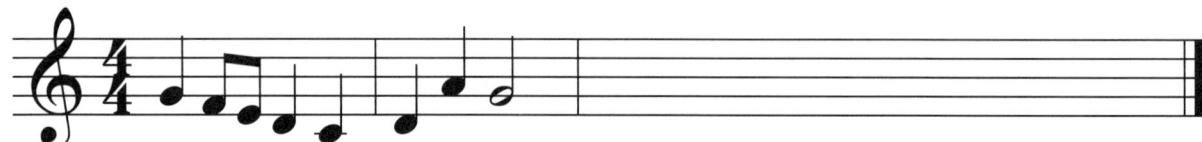

3 Study the following example, then answer the questions below.

The Fifes

Jean François Dandrieu
(1682–1738)

a) Add measure numbers.

b) Add a time signature.

c) Mark any examples of imitation with brackets on the score.

d) Identify the intervals in the treble staff in m. 1 _____ and m. 3 _____ .

Ear-Training Worksheet

LESSON 18

 1 **Interval Identification:** Name the intervals you hear as ↗ min 2, maj 2, min 3, maj 3, P4, P5, maj 6, P8, ↘ maj 2, min 3, P4, P5, or P8.

a)   b)   c)   d)   e)

f)   g)   h)   i)   j)

 2 **Triads:** You will hear a minor triad followed by either the root or the third. Write the note you hear on the staff beside each triad.

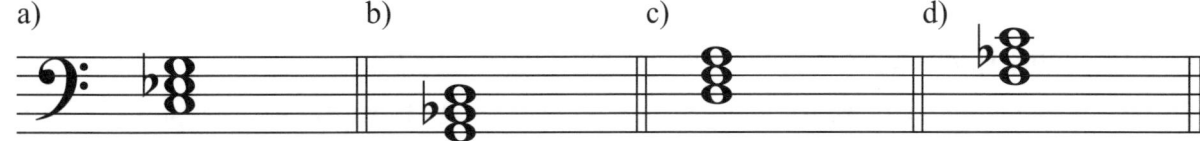

 3 **Rhythmic Dictation:**
  a) Clap the *rhythm* of the melody you hear from memory.
  b) Write it in the space below. The melody is in 2/4 time.

 4 **Melodic Dictation:** Add the missing notes under the bracket. The melody will be played twice.

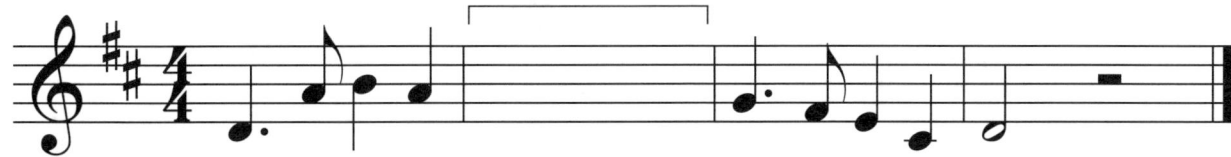

 5 **Melodic Improvisation:** You will hear a two-measure opening.
  a) Improvise a two-measure response.
  b) Write your response on the staff below. Your melody should end on the tonic.

Opening: Response:

Learning Guide

Texture in Music

The word **texture** is used to describe how music is woven together. You can identify a musical texture by listening, or by looking at the music. Texture is one feature you can use to identify when a piece of music was written.

Polyphonic Texture

One type of musical texture is called **polyphonic**: "poly" means "many," and "phonic" means "sound." Music that features two or more melodic lines played together has a polyphonic texture.

The word **counterpoint** is also used to describe this kind of texture.

You have learned that one phrase can imitate another phrase. In **imitative counterpoint,** the melodic lines in a polyphonic texture imitate one another. One familiar example of imitative counterpoint is a **round** or **canon**, such as "Are You Sleeping" ("Frère Jacques").

The following example has two independent melodic parts. Therefore it has a polyphonic texture. It is in imitative counterpoint because the lower part imitates the upper part.

Mixolydian Mix-up

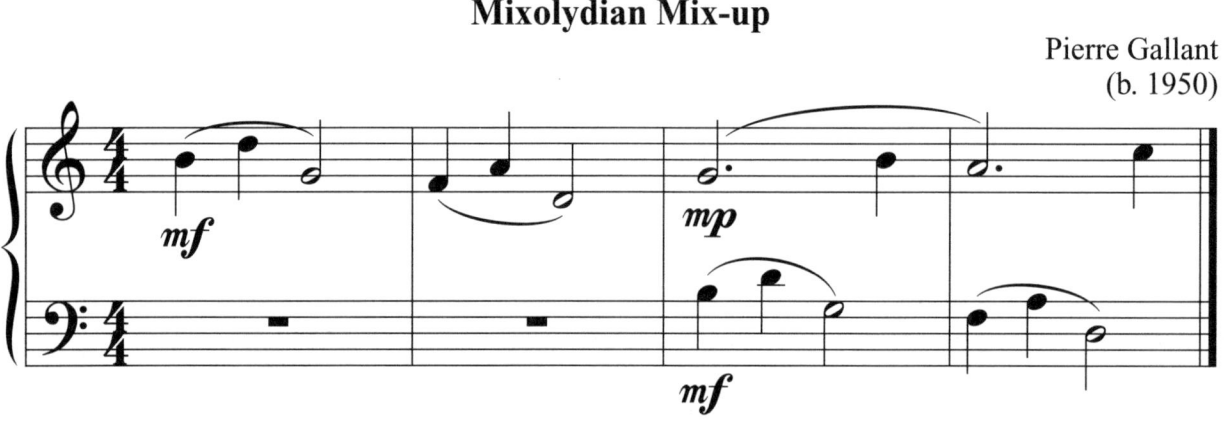

Source: *Imitations and Inventions*
© Copyright 2003 The Frederick Harris Music Co., Limited, Mississauga, Ontario, Canada.

The next example also has a polyphonic texture. It is not in imitative counterpoint because the two independent parts do not imitate each other.

Minuet in Rondo Form

Learning Guide — Lesson 19

Homophonic Texture

Music that features one melodic line with an accompaniment has a **homophonic** texture.

The following example is homophonic; it has a single melody with an accompaniment. The broken-chord figure in the accompaniment is called an **Alberti bass**.

Sonatina in G major

Thomas Attwood
(1765–1838)

The Whole Rest

A whole rest is equal in duration to a whole note or four quarter notes. A whole rest is also used to indicate a whole measure of silence in any meter.

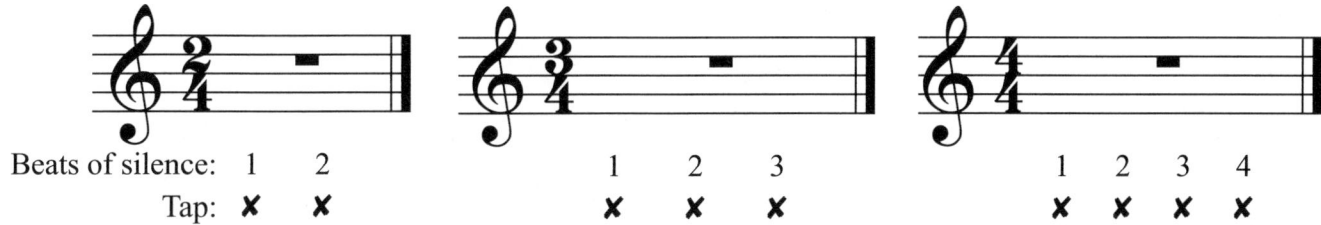

Beats of silence: 1 2   1 2 3   1 2 3 4
Tap: ✗ ✗   ✗ ✗ ✗   ✗ ✗ ✗ ✗

LESSON 19 Theory Worksheet

1 Study the following excerpt, then answer the questions below.

Swirling Leaves

Gordon A. McKinnon (b. 1959)

Andante espressivo

© Copyright 1994 The Frederick Harris Music Co., Limited, Mississauga, Ontario, Canada.

a) Number the measures.

b) Name the composer of this piece. _____

c) How many beats does the rest in the first measure receive? _____

d) Identify the texture of this music. _____

e) In which measure does the lower part begin? _____

2 Study the following excerpt, then answer the questions below.

Study in C major
op. 777, no. 3

Carl Czerny (1791–1857)

Allegro

a) Number the measures.

b) Name the composer of this piece. _____

c) Identify the dynamic marking in m. 1. What does it tell you to do? _____

d) Identify the texture of this music. _____

e) Name the triad played by the left hand in mm. 1 and 2. (Check the clef!) _____

Ear-Training Worksheet

LESSON 19

 1 **Interval Identification:** Name the intervals you hear as ↗ min 2, maj 2, min 3, maj 3, P4, P5, maj 6, P8, ↘ maj 2, min 3, P4, P5, or P8.

a)　　　　b)　　　　c)　　　　d)　　　　e)

f)　　　　g)　　　　h)　　　　i)　　　　j)

 2 **Sight Singing:**
a) Pause the recording. Sing up and down by half steps from C to G.
b) Turn to the answer key and sing along with the recording.

 3 **Rhythmic Dictation:**
a) Clap the *rhythm* of the melody you hear from memory.
b) Write it in the space below. The melody is in 3/4 time.

 4 **Melody Singback/Playback:** Sing the melody you hear from memory, then play it on your instrument. The melody is in B♭ major, 4/4 time.

 5 **Texture Identification:** Identify the texture of the example you hear as polyphonic or homophonic.

a) ❑ polyphonic　　　　b) ❑ polyphonic
　 ❑ homophonic　　　　　 ❑ homophonic

Learning Guide

Consonance and Dissonance

In music, a **consonance** is a sound that has a restful quality. Consonant intervals and chords are pleasing to the ear. They have a "settled" sound that does not seem to need to "resolve."

A **dissonance** is the opposite of a consonance. A dissonant interval or chord has a restless sound. It may seem harsh to the ear. Composers use dissonant intervals and chords to create musical tension.

Dissonance followed by consonance creates resolution.

You can experiment with consonance and dissonance on a keyboard instrument.

1) Play a major 3rd, then a minor 2nd. Which interval sounds more dissonant?
2) Play a solid (blocked) C major triad, then play the notes C-E-G♯ as a chord. Compare the sound of these two chords. Which triad is more consonant?

The Sound of the Major 7th

To memorize the sound of this interval, sing up the major scale from $\hat{1}$ to $\hat{7}$ (do up to ti), then repeat the lowest and highest notes.

The major 7th is a dissonant interval. The dissonance is even more noticeable when you play the two notes of a major 7th together (blocked) on a keyboard.

Turn to the Song Clue Chart on p. 119 and put a ✔ beside the major 7th (maj 7).

Musical Style

In Level 2, you learned that the word "style" is used when defining the unique character of a musical work.

Musical style can be identified by nationality or culture. For example, the music of Spain sounds different from the music of India.

Musical style can also identify when a piece of music was written. For example, the music that composers write today sounds different from music written 200 years ago.

Changes in musical style usually happen gradually, over the course of time. In the past 400 years, there have been four main style periods:

    Baroque (1600–1750)
    Classical (1750–1825)
    Romantic (1825–1900)
    Contemporary (1900–present)

Theory Worksheet

LESSON 20

1. Write notes that are a whole tone above the given notes.

a)   b)   c)   d)   e)

2. Name the following intervals. Remember to think of the major key and scale of the lower note.

a)   b)   c)   d)   e)

___   ___   ___   ___   ___

3. Write the following triads on the staff below in whole notes. Use key signatures.

a)   b)   c)   d)   e)

G major   B♭ major   D major   F major   C major

4. Circle the quarter-note beats. Add bar lines according to the time signature.

Sound Advice Level 3   Lesson 20 Theory Worksheet   91

LESSON 20 Ear-Training Worksheet

1 **Interval Identification:** Identify the intervals you hear as ↗ min 2, maj 2, min 3, maj 3, P4, P5, maj 6, maj 7, P8, ↘ maj 2, min 3, P4, P5, or P8.

a)   b)   c)   d)   e)

f)   g)   h)   i)   j)

2 **Sight Singing:**
a) Pause the recording. Sing up and down by half steps from C to G.
b) Turn to the answer key and sing along with the recording.

3 **Rhythmic Dictation:**
a) Clap the *rhythm* of the melody you hear from memory.
b) Write it in the space below. The melody is in 2/4 time.

4 **Melody Singback/Playback:** Sing the melody you hear from memory, then play it on your instrument. It is in D major, 2/4 time.

I LISTENED ☐ TIMES

5 **Texture Identification:** Identify the texture of the example you hear as polyphonic or homophonic.

a) ❏ polyphonic   b) ❏ polyphonic
  ❏ homophonic   ❏ homophonic

Learning Guide

Expression Markings

If music were performed without any dynamic contrast or expression, it would be very dull, like listening to someone talk without any inflection in his or her voice. Can you imagine saying the statement below without any expression?

"John! Quick! Come and see the fire!"

Composers add words or symbols to their music to tell us how it should sound. These markings are called **expression markings**. Symbols or words that tell us how quickly or slowly to play are called **tempo markings**. Symbols or words that tell us how loudly or softly to play are called **dynamic markings**.

Many expression markings are in Italian. They first appeared in Italy more than 300 years ago, and composers still use them today.

Dynamic Markings

In Level 2, you learned six dynamic markings. Review them in the chart below.

Italian Term	Symbol	Definition
pianissimo	*pp*	very soft
piano	*p*	soft
mezzo piano	*mp*	medium soft
mezzo forte	*mf*	medium loud
forte	*f*	loud
fortissimo	*ff*	very loud

Here are three more dynamic markings. Composers use these markings to tell us that the music should get gradually louder (*crescendo*) or gradually softer (*diminuendo* or *decrescendo*). These marking can cover a few notes, or they can last for several measures.

Learn these three Italian terms with their abbreviations and symbols. In published music, you may also see either abbreviations or symbols.

Italian Term	Abbreviation	Symbol	Definition
crescendo	*cresc.*	⟨	gradually getting louder
decrescendo	*decresc.*	⟩	gradually getting softer
diminuendo	*dim.*	⟩	gradually getting softer

Sound Advice Level 3   Lesson 21 Learning Guide

LESSON 21 Theory Worksheet

1 Match each Italian term with its definition by writing the appropriate letter in the empty box.

piano	
forte	
mezzo piano	
fortissimo	
decrescendo	
diminuendo	
pianissimo	

a) loud
b) very loud
c) gradually getting softer
d) very soft
e) medium soft
f) gradually getting softer
g) soft

2 Draw a line to connect each of the following time signatures with its correct accent pattern.

3 Memorize all the terms and symbols in the Terms and Symbols Chart on pp. 117–118. This chart also includes terms and symbols covered in Levels 1 and 2.

4 Write an F major scale, ascending and descending, using accidentals.

5 Write a B♭ major scale, ascending and descending, using accidentals.

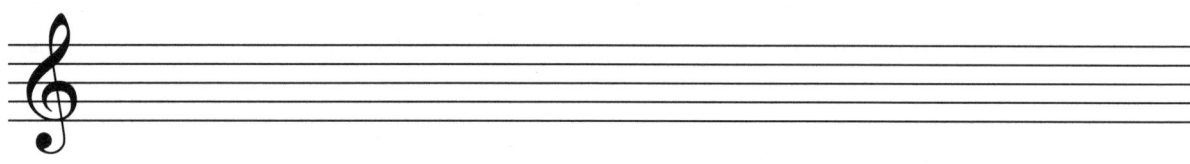

Theory Worksheet — Lesson 21

6 Complete the following chart by filling in the blanks with one *dotted* note.

♩ ♩ ♩	=	
𝅗𝅥 𝅗𝅥 𝅗𝅥	=	
♬ ♬ ♬ (sixteenths)	=	
♪ ♪ ♪	=	

7 Complete the following chart by filling in the blanks with *one* note.

𝅗𝅥	+		=	𝅗𝅥.
♪	+		=	♪.
o	+		=	o.
♩	+		=	♩.

LESSON 21 Ear-Training Worksheet

1 **Interval Identification:** The first note of each interval is given. Name the interval you hear and write the second note.

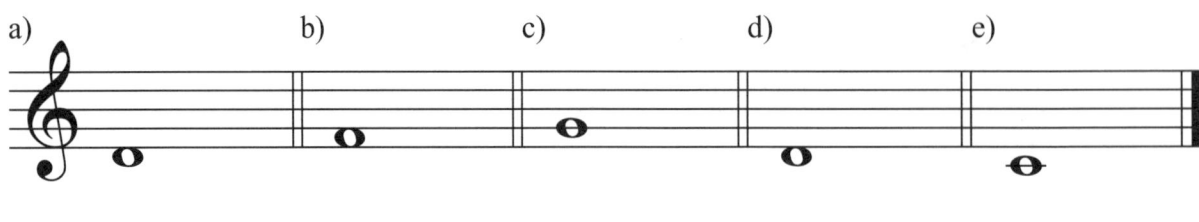

2 **Melodic Improvisation:** You will hear a two-measure opening.
a) Improvise a two-measure response.
b) Write your response on the staff below. Your melody should end on the tonic.

3 **Rhythmic Dictation:**
a) Sing, tap, or clap the rhythm you hear from memory.
b) Write it in the space below. The rhythm is in $\frac{4}{4}$ time.

4 **Error Detection:** Compare the melody you hear with the melody written below, and circle any differences. Rewrite the melody as it was played on the recording.

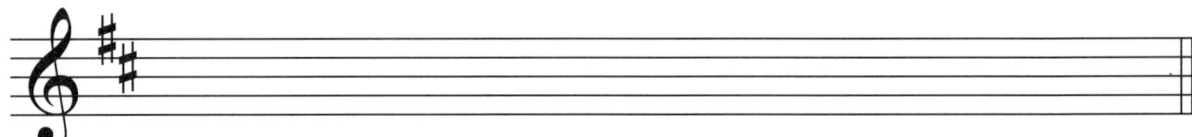

5 **Texture Identification:** Identify the texture of the example you hear as polyphonic or homophonic.

a) ❏ polyphonic   b) ❏ polyphonic
    ❏ homophonic   ❏ homophonic

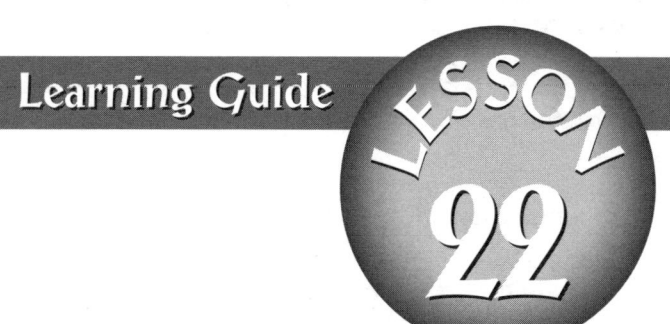

Learning Guide

Review of Baroque Style

In Level 2, you learned about musical style during the Baroque period (1600–1750). This music was written between 300 and 400 years ago. Here are four important features of Baroque musical style:

- polyphonic texture
- melodic imitation
- terraced dynamics
- dance forms

Musical Style of the Classical Period

The Classical period (1750–1825) is a little closer to the present time. Music of the Classical period was written about 200–250 years ago. Here are four important features of Classical musical style:

Homophonic Texture
One of the most obvious differences between Baroque and Classical styles is the texture. While Baroque music is largely polyphonic, Classical music is generally homophonic (one melodic line with an accompaniment).

Crescendo and Diminuendo
Baroque composers used terraced dynamics (contrasts of loud and soft). Composers of the Classical period often changed dynamic levels gradually by using *crescendo* and *diminuendo* markings. They especially liked to use a *crescendo* as the music builds to an exciting climax.

Symmetrical Phrasing
In Baroque music, it is sometimes hard to hear the cadences because of the polyphonic texture and the melodic imitation. In Classical music, the phrases are much more symmetrical, with cadences occurring at predictable points. For example, a four-measure phrase may be answered by another four-measure phrase, an eight-measure phrase will be answered by another eight-measure phrase, and so on.

Absolute Music: Sonatas, Symphonies, and Sonatinas
Music that does not have a descriptive title is called **absolute music**. In Classical music, instrumental works typically have titles like these:

Sonata in F Major
Symphony No. 5 in C Minor
Sonatina No. 3 in G Major

Classical music can be very expressive and have a wide range of moods. However, words such as *sonata* and *symphony* do not indicate a story or picture that the composer may have had in mind when writing the music. As performers or listeners we create these images ourselves. Most of the instrumental music from the Classical period is absolute music.

Titles such as sonata, sonatina, and symphony do not describe a mood or image, but they do tell us about the structure—or form—of the music.

LESSON 22 Learning Guide

A **sonata** has three or four long sections called **movements**. Each movement has a different mood or character, and a different tempo. Classical composers wrote sonatas for various kinds of instruments, including piano, violin, flute, clarinet, and cello.

A **symphony** is similar to a sonata, but it is written for an orchestra. Most symphonies written in the Classical period have four movements.

A **sonatina** is a shorter version of a sonata. Sonatinas usually have three movements and are written for piano.

Keyboard Instruments in the Classical Period

The pianos that appeared toward the end of the Baroque period were called *fortepianos* because they could produce both loud and soft sounds. During the Classical period, the *fortepiano* quickly became the most popular keyboard instrument. Harpsichords and clavichords were still available, but most composers and performers preferred the piano because dynamic shadings could be controlled by the player's touch. A typical piano from this period had a wooden frame and thin strings. It had a light action and produced a clearer, more delicate tone than the modern grand. Today's pianos have a cast-iron frame and more strings, and can produce a much louder, more brilliant sound than the early intruments.

Theory Worksheet — Lesson 22

1 a) Sing or play the following two-measure melodic opening, then improvise a response. Your response should end on the tonic.

b) Write your response on the staff.

2 The following excerpt is the opening of the third movement of a sonatina. Study the music, then answer the questions below.

a) Name the key. _____

b) Write the time signature and the measure numbers on the score.

c) What are the composer's dates? _____

d) Which staff contains the melody? _____

e) Is the texture of this music polyphonic or homophonic? _____

f) What do the bass-clef notes in m. 1 create? _____

g) What do the treble-clef notes in mm. 1–2 create? _____

h) In which style period do you think this music was written? _____

LESSON 22: Ear-Training Worksheet

1. Interval Identification: The first note of each interval is given. Name the interval and write the second note.

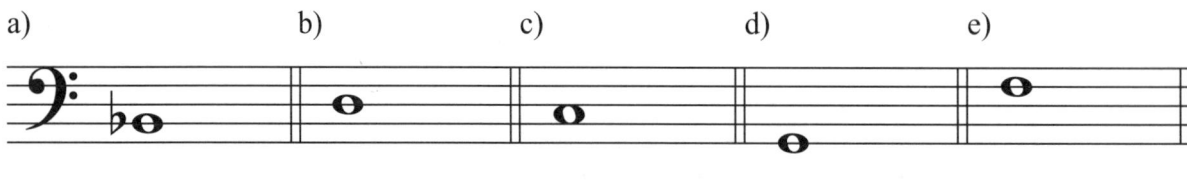

2. Melodic Improvisation: You will hear a two-measure opening.
a) Improvise a two-measure response.
b) Write your response on the staff below. Your melody should end on the tonic.

3. Rhythmic Dictation: Sing, tap, or clap the rhythmic pattern you hear from memory, then write it in the space below. The rhythm is in $\frac{4}{4}$ time.

4. Error Detection: Compare the melody you hear with the melody written below, and circle any differences. Rewrite the melody as it was played on the recording.

Menuetto

Wolfgang Amadeus Mozart
(1756–1791)

5. Texture Identification: Identify the texture of the example you hear as polyphonic or homophonic.

a) ❏ polyphonic
   ❏ homophonic

b) ❏ polyphonic
   ❏ homophonic

Learning Guide

The Orchestra

Orchestras have changed considerably over the course of music history. The modern symphony orchestra is much larger and louder than an orchestra of the Baroque period or the Classical period. The orchestra developed gradually over time, as new or improved instruments provided a richer and fuller sound. Today, composers have a wide range of dynamics and tone colors at their fingertips.

The Baroque Orchestra

The orchestra of the Baroque period was quite small. It consisted mainly of stringed instruments. Often, Baroque composers included several woodwind instruments (flutes, oboes, bassoons). Occasionally they added brass instruments (trumpets, horns). The harpsichord was also an important part of Baroque ensembles.

Baroque orchestras did not have a conductor standing on a podium. Instead, the harpsichordist or the first violinist directed the ensemble while playing.

The Classical Orchestra

During the Classical period, the orchestra developed into four standard sections or "families" of instruments: strings, woodwinds, brass, and percussion. The harpsichord was not usually part of the Classical orchestra. A Classical orchestra usually had from twenty-five to forty members. This is still quite small compared to later orchestras that had as many as one hundred players.

As the orchestra grew in size, it became more difficult for the musicians to see each other and keep together. Most performances during the Classical period were led by a conductor who stood in front of the orchestra. Classical composers often conducted their own music.

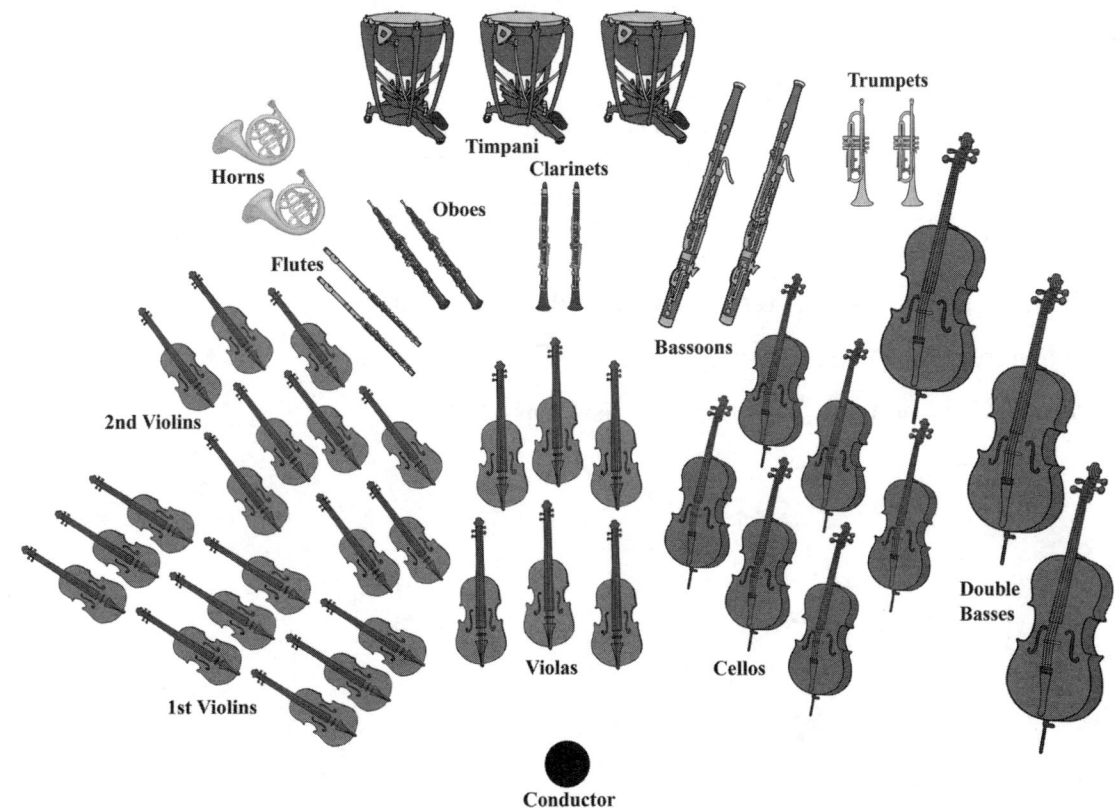

Sound Advice Level 3 Lesson 23 Learning Guide

Theory Worksheet

1.
a) Sing or play the following two-measure melodic opening, then improvise a response. Your response should imitate the first measure and end on the tonic.

b) Write your response on the staff.

2. The following excerpt is the opening of the third movement of a sonatina. Study the music, then answer the questions below.

a) What is the difference between a sonatina and a sonata? _____

b) What are the composer's dates? _____

c) What does ♩ = 108 – 116 tell you? _____

d) Name the two different ways the notes are played in the right hand. _____

e) Do the notes in the treble clef create a melody that could stand on its own? _____

f) Do the notes in the bass clef create a melody that could stand on its own? _____

g) Is the texture of this music polyphonic or homophonic? _____

h) In which style period do you think this music was written? _____

Ear-Training Worksheet

LESSON 23

1 **Interval Identification:** Identify the intervals you hear as ↗ min 2, maj 2, min 3, maj 3, P4, P5, maj 6, maj 7, P8, ↘ maj 2, min 3, P4, P5, or P8.

a)   b)   c)   d)   e)

f)   g)   h)   i)   j)

2 **Sight Singing:**
a) Pause the recording. Sing the following melody while you tap a steady quarter-note beat.
b) Turn to the answer key and sing along with the recording.

3 **Melodic Dictation:**
a) Sing the melody you hear from memory.
a) Write it on the staff below. The melody is in F major, in 3/4 time.

I LISTENED ☐ TIMES

4 **Triads:** You will hear a major triad followed by either its root or its third. Write the note you hear on the staff beside each triad.

a)   b)   c)   d)

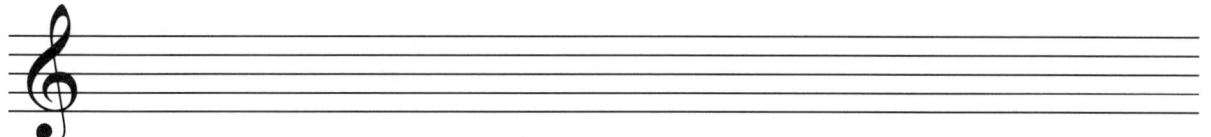

5 **Texture Identification:** Identify the texture of the example you hear as polyphonic or homophonic.

a) ☐ polyphonic   b) ☐ polyphonic
   ☐ homophonic   ☐ homophonic

Composers of the Classical Period

In the Classical period, Vienna was an important city for music making. Vienna is the largest city in Austria.

Franz Joseph Haydn (1732–1809)

Haydn was born in Austria but spent most of his career in nearby Hungary as the court composer for the wealthy and powerful Esterházy family. The Esterházy estate had its own orchestra, opera company, and chapel.

Haydn wrote more than a hundred symphonies, dozens of piano sonatas, and many chamber and choral works. His music often contains humor. For example, the "Surprise Symphony" has a loud chord that was supposed to wake up the audience if they had fallen asleep.

Wolfgang Amadeus Mozart (1756–1791)

Mozart was born in Salzburg, Austria. He was a child prodigy, and was already composing at age five. His father, Leopold Mozart, took young Wolfgang and his sister, Nannerl, on concert tours all over Europe.

Mozart's music has an elegant sound. He wrote music of all types but he especially loved opera. Unlike Haydn, Mozart did not like working at court. Instead, he moved to Vienna to make a living on his own, but he was not financially successful. When he died, at age thirty-five, he was living in poverty.

Ludwig van Beethoven (1770–1827)

Beethoven was born in Bonn, Germany but spent most of his career in Vienna. Like Haydn and Mozart, he wrote choral and instrumental music. He wrote in the Classical forms but greatly expanded them in length and emotional force. Publishers were eager to print and sell Beethoven's music, and wealthy music lovers gave him financial support.

Beethoven began to lose his hearing early in his career, but he continued to compose even after he was completely deaf. He was admired during his lifetime and was in frequent demand as a performer and composer. Thousands of people attended his funeral.

Franz Schubert (1797–1828)

Schubert was born in Vienna and, like Mozart, died at an early age. His music bridges the Classical and Romantic eras and has characteristics of both style periods. Most of Schubert's symphonies and piano sonatas are in the Classical style, but his songs are more Romantic. You will learn more about Schubert in Level 4.

Theory Worksheet — Lesson 24

1 Study the following excerpt, then answer the questions below.

Menuetto in D Major

Wolfgang Amadeus Mozart
(1756–1791)

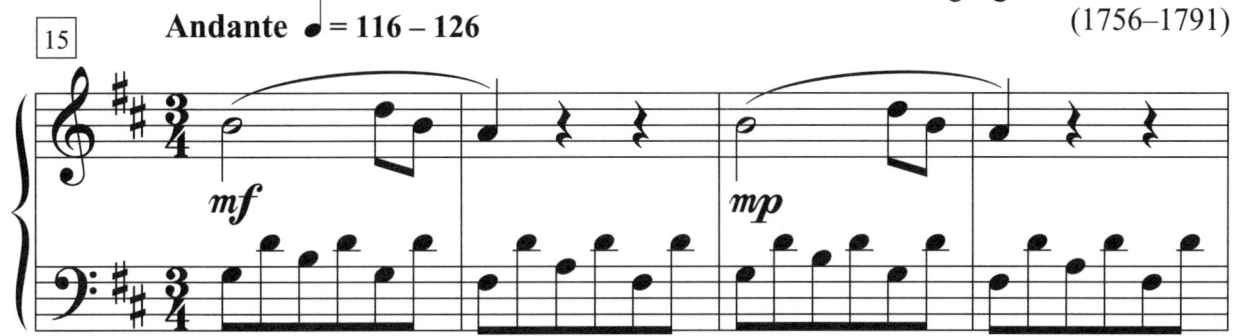

Key: _____

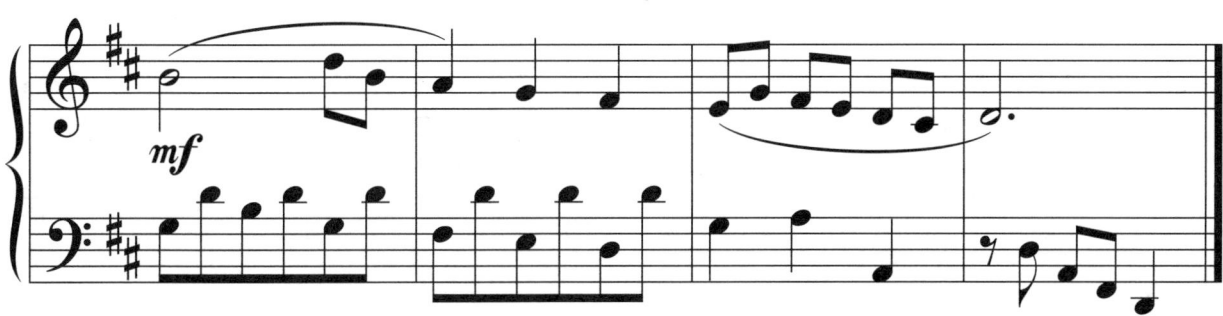

a) Name the key and number the measures. (This excerpt starts on m. 15.)

b) Draw a bracket over any examples of imitation.

c) What are the composer's dates? _____

d) Name the triad in the bass staff in m. 15. _____

e) What does the dynamic marking in m. 19 tell you to do? _____

f) What do the notes in the bass staff in m. 22 create? _____

g) Is the texture of this music homophonic or polyphonic? _____

h) In which style period do you think this music was written? _____

2 Listen to an orchestral piece composed by Mozart, Haydn, or Beethoven. (Better yet, go to a concert!) Write down the name of the piece that you listened to. Your teacher will be able to suggest works that you would enjoy.

LESSON 24
Ear-Training Worksheet

 1 **Interval Identification:** Identify the intervals you hear as ↗ min 2, maj 2, min 3, maj 3, P4, P5, maj 6, maj 7, P8, ↘ maj 2, min 3, P4, P5, or P8.

    a)   b)   c)   d)   e)

    f)   g)   h)   i)   j)

 2 **Triads:** You will hear a major triad followed by either its root or its third. Write the note you hear on the staff beside the triad.

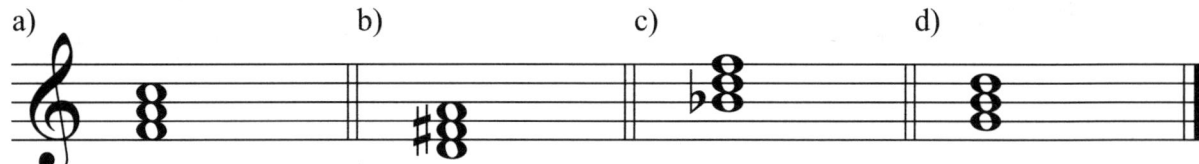

 3 **Rhythmic Dictation:**
    a) Clap the *rhythm* of the melody you hear from memory.
    b) Write it in the space below. The melody is in 3/4 time.

 4 **Melodic Dictation:**
    a) Sing the melody you hear from memory.
    b) Write it on the staff below. The melody is in D major, in 3/4 time.

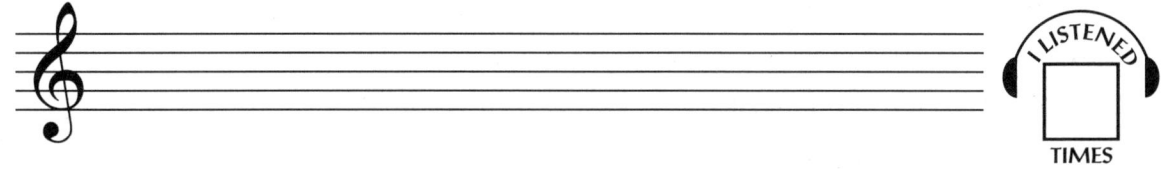

 5 **Error Detection:** Compare the melody you hear with the melody written below, and circle any differences. Rewrite the melody as it was played on the recording.

German Dance

Franz Joseph Haydn
(1732–1809)

Theory Examination

Duration: one hour

Name: _____

6 **1** Name the following notes.

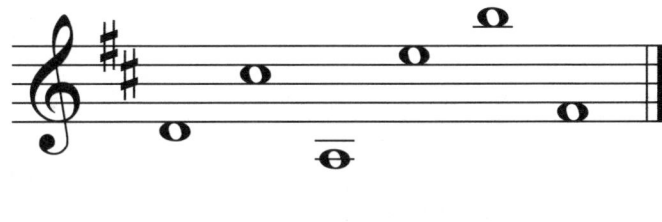

___ ___ ___ ___ ___

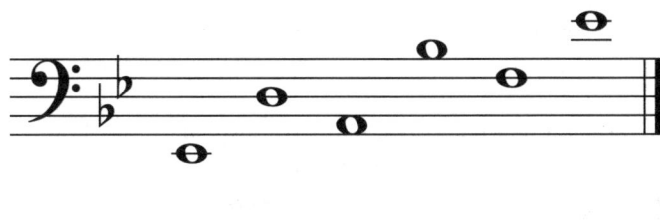

___ ___ ___ ___ ___

4 **2** Write the following key signatures.

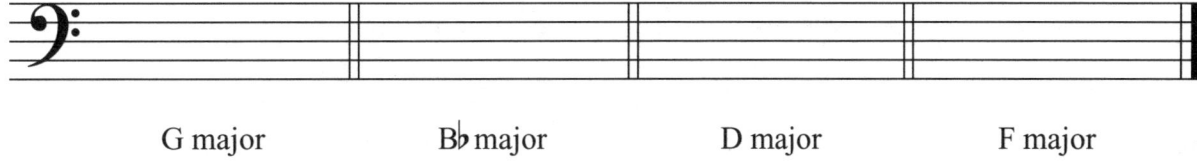

6 **3** Using accidentals, write the following solid (blocked) triads on the staff below.

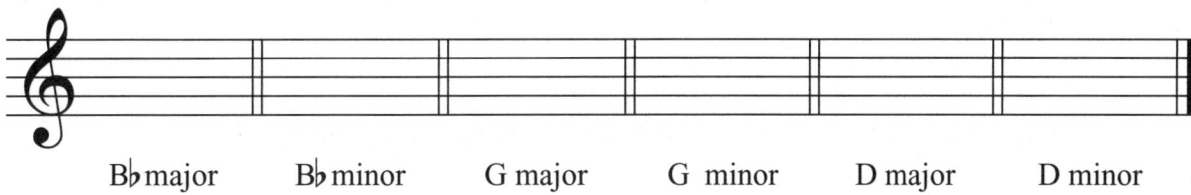

6 **4** Name the following intervals.

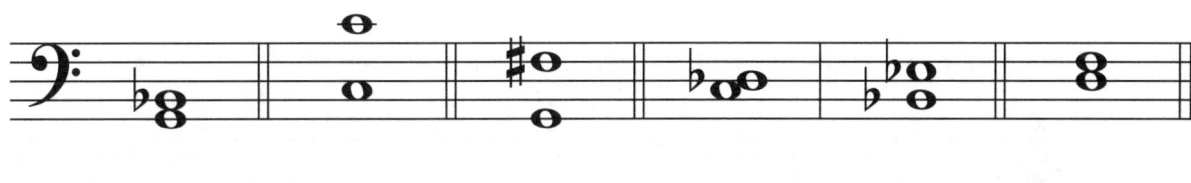

___ ___ ___ ___ ___

Sound Advice Level 3   Theory Examination   107

Theory Examination

6 **5** Draw a line from each term on the left to its correct definition on the right.

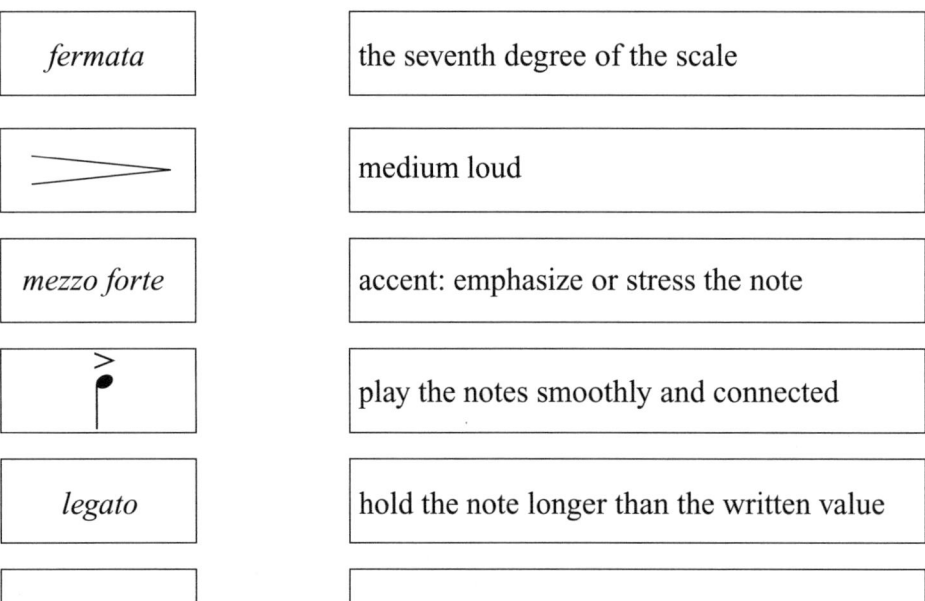

4 **6** Circle the quarter-note beats. Add bar lines according to the time signature.

6 **7** a) Write a D major scale, ascending and descending, using a key signature.

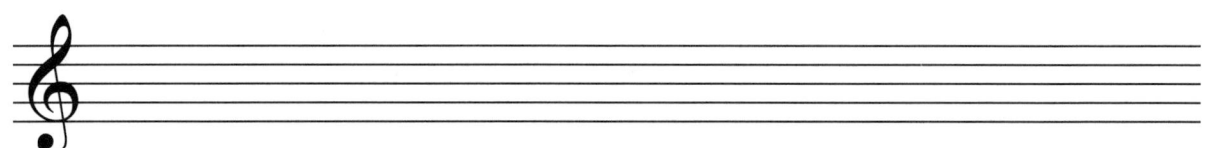

b) Write a B♭ major scale, ascending and descending, using accidentals.

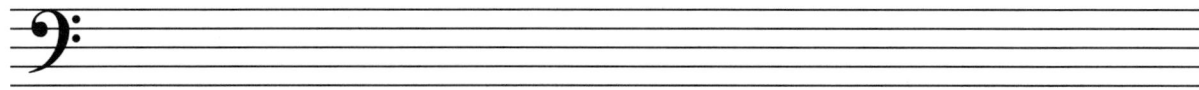

c) Write an F major scale, descending only, using a key signature.

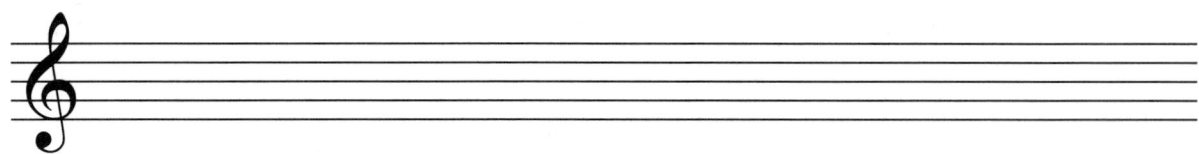

Theory Examination

2 **8)** Write the names of the notes on the blank lines below.

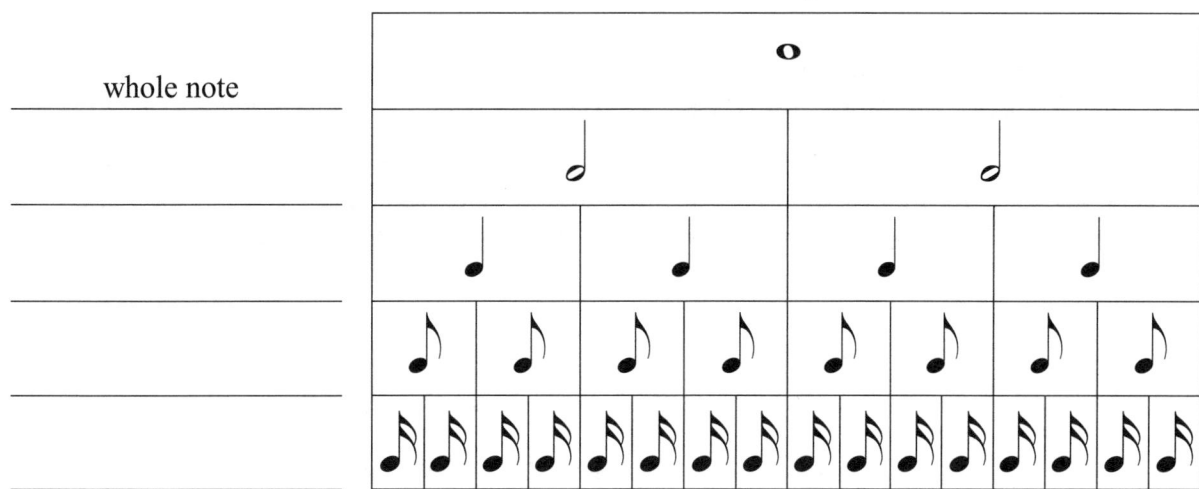

Note-Value Comparison Chart

whole note

4 **9)** Complete the following chart by filling in each blank with a number.

There are		sixteenth notes in an eighth note.
There are		eighth notes in a quarter note.
There are		quarter notes in a half note.
There are		half notes in a whole note.
There are		eighth notes in a half note.
There are		quarter notes in a dotted half note.
There are		eighth notes in a dotted quarter note.
There are		sixteenth notes in a dotted eighth note.

2 **10)** Rewrite the following example, beaming the notes to show the quarter-note beats. Add bar lines.

$\frac{4}{4}$

4 **11)** a) Sing the following two-measure opening, then improvise your own response.

b) When you are happy with your response, write it in the space below. Your response should imitate the first measure and end on the tonic.

50

Sound Advice Level 3 — Theory Examination — 109

Melody Master

These are the final Ear-Training Worksheets for Level 3. Spend as much time as necessary to perfect these assignments. When you finish Melody Master, you are ready to move on to *Sound Advice* Level 4.

Melody Master consists of five sets of melodies. You need to complete all five sets using the three different methods described below. Finish all five sets with Method 1 before you go on to Method 2. Finish the five sets with Method 2 before you move on to Method 3. When you successfully complete each set, check the box at the bottom of this page to track your progress.

Always record your progress before going on to the next method!

Method 1: Melody Playback—Play What You Hear

Singers and instrumentalists can perform in their range. Each melody will be played twice on the recordings. The tonic (do) and the beat are given before each performance. The melodies start on either the first or the third note of the scale.

Method 2: Sight Singing—Hear What You See

Turn to the Melody Master Answer Key and sight sing all five sets.

Method 3: Melodic Dictation—Write What You Hear

Write each melody on the staff. Each melody will be played twice. The tonic (do) and the beat are given before each performance. The melodies start on either the first or the third note of the scale.

Method 1: Playbacks		Method 2: Sight Singing		Method 3: Melodic Dictation	
Set One	❏	Set One	❏	Set One	❏
Set Two	❏	Set Two	❏	Set Two	❏
Set Three	❏	Set Three	❏	Set Three	❏
Set Four	❏	Set Four	❏	Set Four	❏
Set Five	❏	Set Five	❏	Set Five	❏

Melody Master

Set One

a) The following melody is in C major, in 4/4 time.

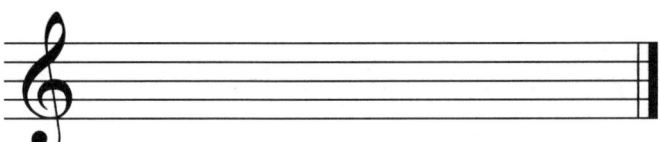

b) The following melody is in F major, in 3/4 time.

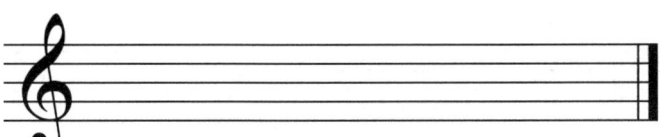

c) The following melody is in G major, in 2/4 time.

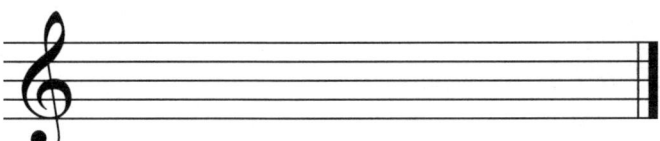

d) The following melody is in D major, in 4/4 time.

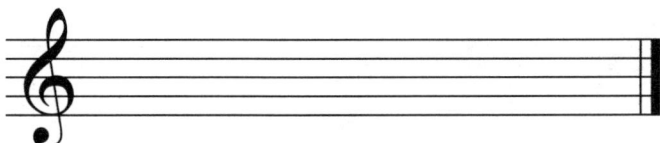

e) The following melody is in B♭ major, in 3/4 time.

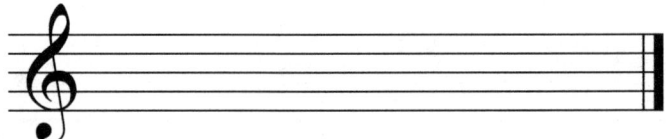

Check the appropriate box on p. 110.

Set Two

a) The following melody is in C major, in 3/4 time.

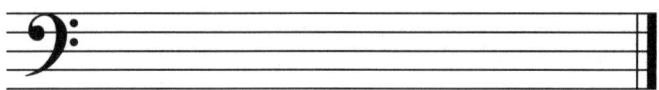

b) The following melody is in D major, in 3/4 time.

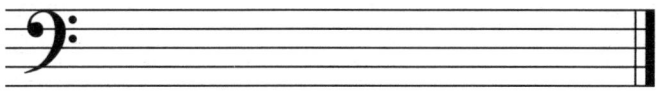

c) The following melody is in F major, in 4/4 time.

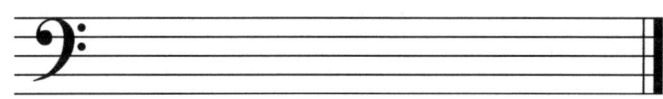

d) The following melody is in G major, in 3/4 time.

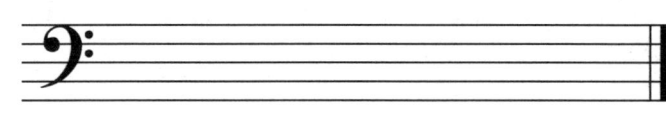

e) The following melody is in B♭ major, in 4/4 time.

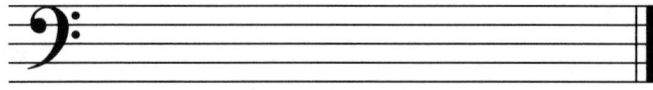

Check the appropriate box on p. 110.

Melody Master

Set Three

a) The following melody is in C major, in 3/4 time.

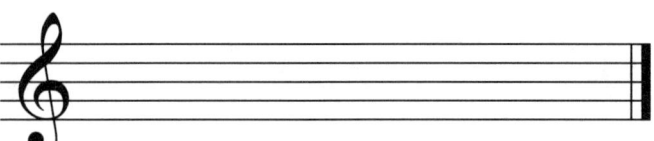

b) The following melody is in F major, in 4/4 time.

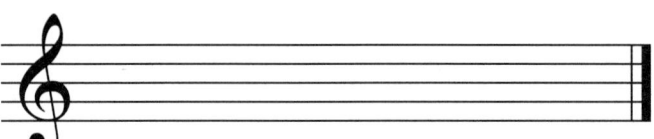

c) The following melody is in G major, in 4/4 time.

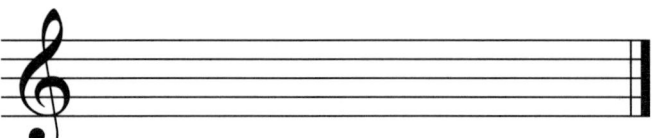

d) The following melody is in B♭ major, in 3/4 time.

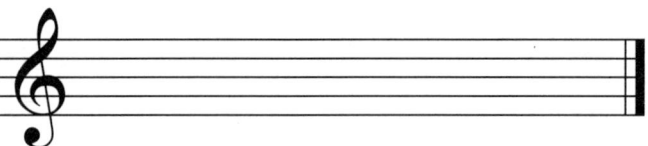

e) The following melody is in C major, in 4/4 time.

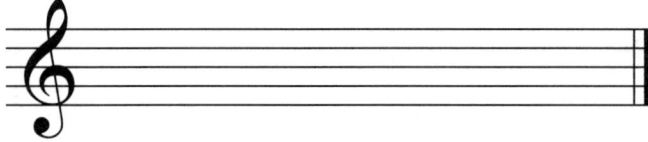

Check the appropriate box on p. 110.

Set Four

a) The following melody is in C major, in 2/4 time.

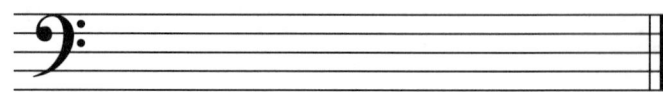

b) The following melody is in B♭ major, in 2/4 time.

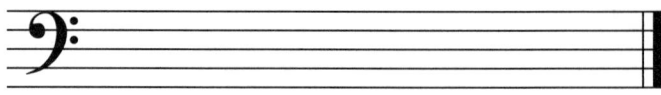

c) The following melody is in F major, in 2/4 time.

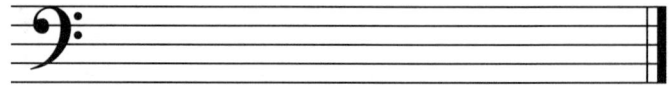

d) The following melody is in G major, in 2/4 time.

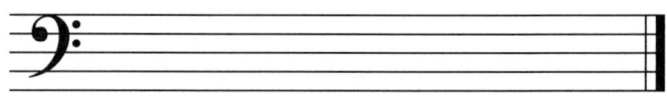

e) The following melody is in D major, in 2/4 time.

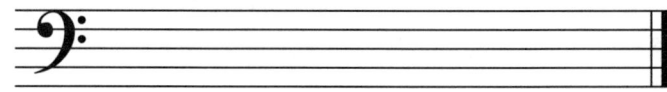

Check the appropriate box on p. 110.

Melody Master

Set Five

a) The following melody is in G major, in 4/4 time.

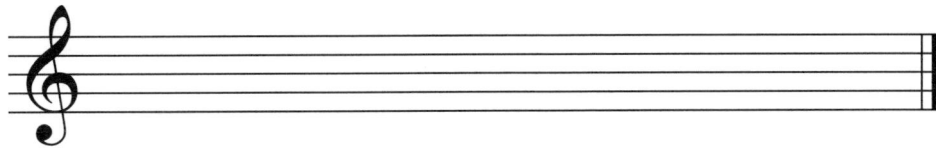

b) The following melody is in F major, in 2/4 time.

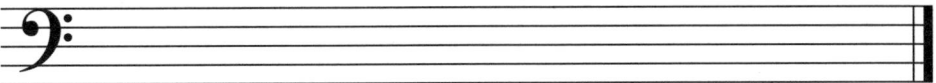

c) The following melody is in C major, in 3/4 time.

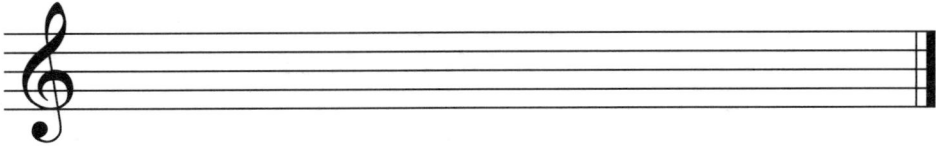

d) The following melody is in D major, in 3/4 time.

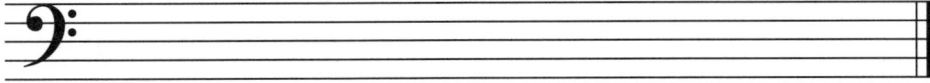

e) The following melody is in B♭ major, in 4/4 time.

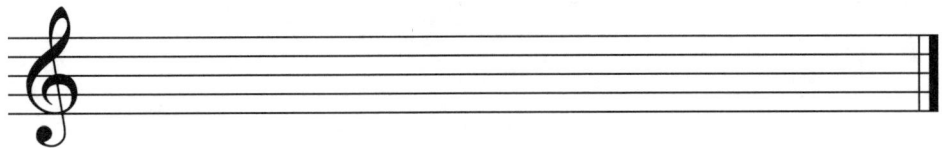

Check the appropriate box on p. 110.

Charts and Games

Drawing Symbols Chart

This chart provides additional space for you to practice drawing various musical symbols. As new symbols are introduced in the lessons, you will be instructed to turn to this chart to practice drawing them.

Practice writing and the following clefs, accidentals, and rests.

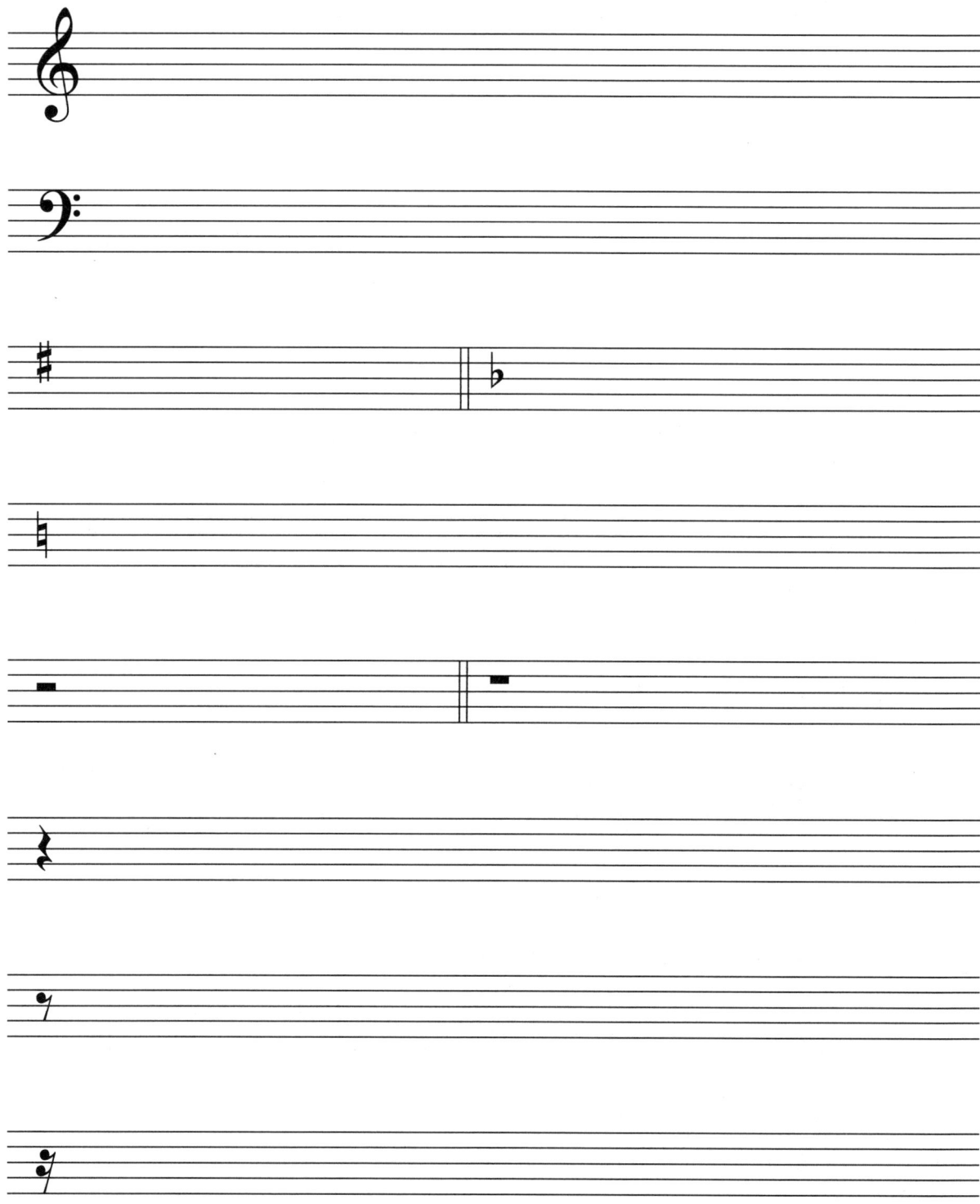

Charts and Games

Rhythm Jumble Chart

Each time you learn a new rhythmic unit, circle it on the Rhythm Jumble Chart.

One-Minute Rhythm Jumble
Use the Rhythm Jumble Chart to practice singing the circled rhythmic units for *one minute* every day. Tap the beat with your finger as you point to the rhythmic unit you are singing. Sing each unit two or three times before moving on to the next one. Gradually mix up the units by randomly pointing to different units. Try not to miss a beat!

You can also use this chart to play any of the Rhythm Jumble games described on the next page.

Sound Advice Level 3 — Charts and Games — 115

Charts and Games

Rhythm Jumble Games

Rhythm Jumble Reading
The goal of this sight-reading game is to sing all the circled rhythmic units on the Rhythm Jumble Chart in random order, while keeping a steady beat. To play Rhythm Jumble Reading, you will need someone to keep track of the number of units you can sing correctly without stopping. You win the game when you can sing at least one more unit than the last time you played. Record your score in the Rhythm Jumble score boxes on your Theory Worksheets. When you can sing 30 units correctly, you will earn the official title of Rhythm Jumble "Reading Expert" and you may write the letters "RE" in the score box.

The rules are:
1) Tap a steady beat with your finger.
2) Point to each rhythmic unit as you sing it.
3) Sing a unit only twice before you move to a new one.
4) Sing the units in random order.
5) You are "out" if you sing a unit incorrectly, or if your steady beat falters.

As you become more proficient, you can make the Rhythm Jumble game more challenging by increasing the tempo. You can also change rule 3 so that you sing a unit only *once* before you move on to the next one. (Students attending group classes can play this game in teams and adapt the rules to meet their needs.)

Rhythm Jumble Solitaire
The rules for Rhythm Jumble Solitaire are the same as for Rhythm Jumble Reading except that you can play without a helper. All you need is a timer. Keep track of the number of seconds that you can continuously sing the rhythmic units in random order before you make a mistake or your steady beat falters. You win the game when you have increased your time from your previous score. Record your scores in the Rhythm Jumble score boxes on your Theory Worksheets. When you can sing random units continuously for one minute, you will have earned the official title of Rhythm Jumble "Solitaire Expert" and you may write the letters "SE" in the score box on your Theory Worksheets.

Rhythm Jumble Composer
To play Rhythm Jumble Composer, you need to make a set of rhythm cards. Use the rhythmic units on the Rhythm Jumble Chart (p. 115). Draw each rhythmic unit on a blank card. Make two copies of each unit. You should have a total of 30 cards.

Compose your own rhythmic pattern by laying out a series of cards from left to right in any order you choose. You can also shuffle the cards to mix them up before laying them out. Tap a steady beat while you point to each card in turn and sing your new rhythmic pattern. Keep track of how many cards you can sing correctly without faltering in your steady beat. Record your score in the boxes on the theory worksheets. When you can correctly sing a pattern that uses all 30 cards, you will earn the official title of Rhythm Jumble "Composing Expert" and you may write the letters "CE" in the score box on your Theory Worksheets.

Charts and Games

Terms and Symbols Chart

This chart lists definitions for all the terms and symbols covered in this volume.

Dynamic Markings

Italian Term	Symbol	Definition
pianissimo	**pp**	very soft
piano	**p**	soft
mezzo piano	**mp**	medium soft
mezzo forte	**mf**	medium loud
forte	**f**	loud
fortissimo	**ff**	very loud

Italian Term	Abbreviation	Symbol	Definition
crescendo	*cresc.*	&lt;	gradually getting louder
decrescendo	*decresc.*	&gt;	gradually getting softer
diminuendo	*dim.*	&gt;	gradually getting softer

Charts and Games

Miscellaneous Terms and Symbols

Term	Symbols	Definition
staccato		short and detached
legato		smooth and connected
slur		play the notes *legato*
tie		hold for combined value of the tied notes
accent		emphasize or stress
fermata	𝆒	hold the note longer than the written value
da capo al fine	D.C. al Fine	go back to the beginning and play until the *Fine* (end)
metronome marking	M.M. ♩ = 60	a mechanical device that ticks a set number of times each minute so you can determine the tempo
repeat sign		repeat from the beginning
repeat signs		repeat the material within the repeat signs

Charts and Games

Song Clue Chart

This chart shows ascending and descending intervals and provides several song clue examples for each one. There is also space for you to add your own song clues. Each time you learn a new interval you will be instructed to turn to this chart to put a check beside the interval.

Ascending Intervals ↗	✔	Possible Song Clues	Your Own Clues
min 2		Oh, Danny Boy Theme from *The Pink Panther* The Entertainer	
maj 2		Are You Sleeping? Yankee Doodle "Do, a Deer" from *The Sound of Music*	
min 3		Brahms' Lullaby Oh, Canada Greensleeves/What Child Is This?	
maj 3		Oh, When the Saints Go Marching In For He's a Jolly Good Fellow Theme from *Harry Potter*	
P4		Bridal Song ("Here Comes the Bride") We Wish You a Merry Christmas Theme from *Hockey Night in Canada*	
P5		Twinkle, Twinkle, Little Star Lavender's Blue Theme from *Star Wars*	
maj 6		My Bonnie Lies over the Ocean "Colors of the Wind" from *Pocahontas* Jingle Bells ("Dashing Through the Snow")	
P8		Sing a Song of Sixpence Somewhere, Over the Rainbow Let It Snow ("Oh, the weather outside…")	
Descending Intervals ↘		**Possible Song Clues**	**Your Own Clues**
min 3		Star Spangled Banner Rain, Rain, Go Away Ring around the Rosie	
P4		*Eine kleine Nachtmusik* Oh Come, All Ye Faithful Organ music played at hockey games!	
P5		Minuet in G Theme from *The Flintstones*	
P8		Hot Cross Buns Jump, Jive, and Wail	

Charts and Games

Mad Music Game

This timed interval-reading game uses the interval sheet on p. 121. The goal is to name all the intervals on a sheet in two minutes or less. Once you can name all the major and minor 2nds within two minutes, you will have earned the status of "2nds Expert" for Level 3 and will be awarded the certificate of achievement (on the inside back cover).

The easiest way to play Mad Music is to have someone follow the answer sheet while you name the 2nds out loud.

Beginning with Lesson 9, you will often be asked to record three Mad Music scores on your Theory Worksheet. This means that part of your homework assignment for that lesson is to play Mad Music at least three times. Once you have mastered the interval sheet, you do not have to record any more Mad Music scores.

Charts and Games

Mad Music Chart

Name the 2nds (major or minor).

Sound Advice Level 3

Answer Keys

Lesson 1

1 Rhythmic Reading:

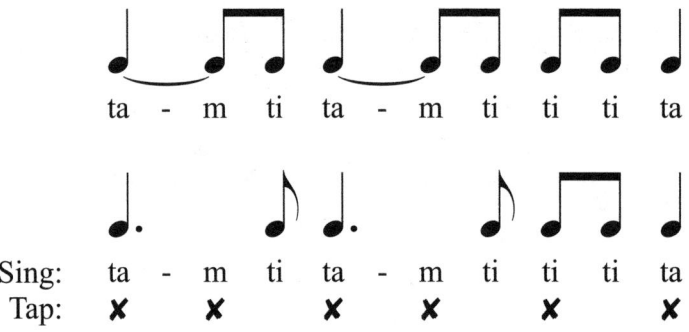

2 Rhythmic Reading:

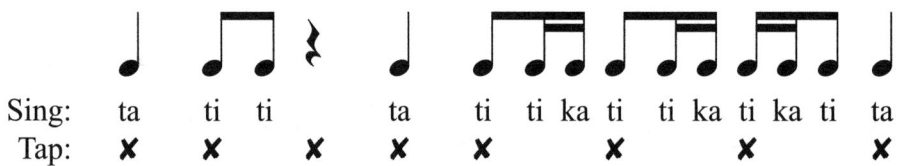

3 Rhythm Singback/Clapback:

4 Rhythm Singback/Clapback:

5 Rhythmic Identification:

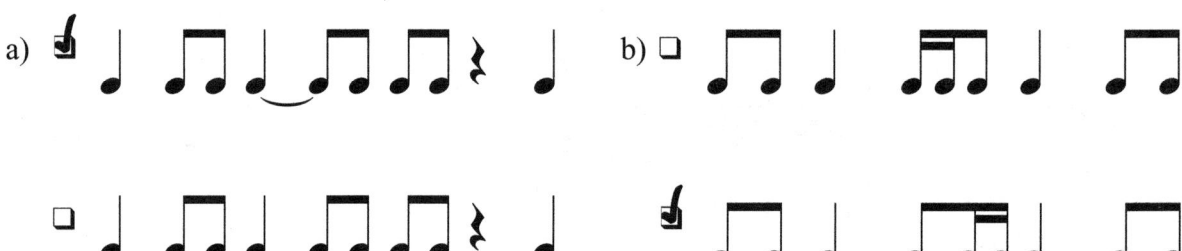

Ear-Training Answer Key

Lesson 2

 1 Editing:

 2 Melodic Identification:

a)

b)

 3 Rhythmic Identification:

a)

b)

4 Rhythm Singback/Clapback:

Ear-Training Answer Key

Lesson 3

 1 Rhythmic Reading:

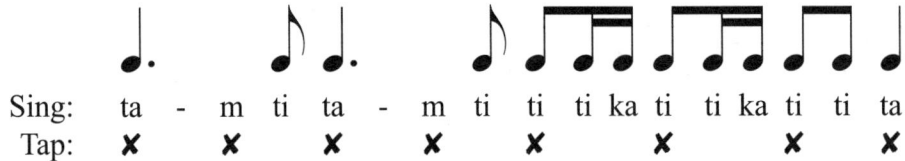

 2 Rhythmic Identification:

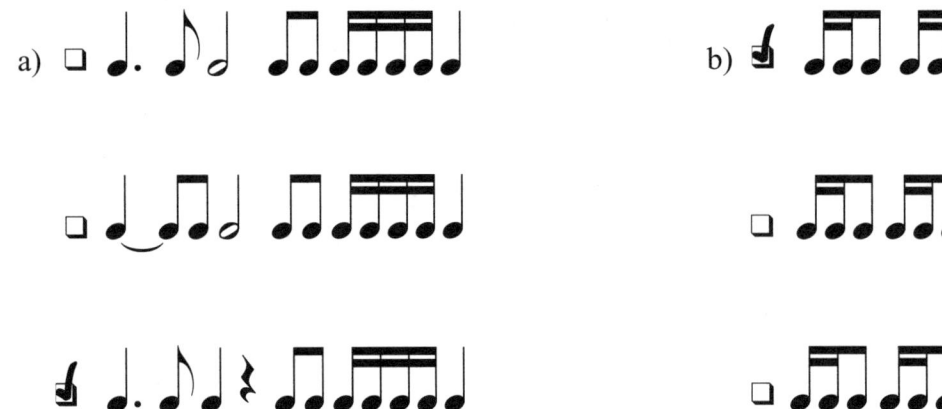

 3 Rhythm Singback/Clapback:

 4 Rhythmic Dictation:

 5 Editing:

Ear-Training Answer Key

Lesson 4

1 Rhythmic Reading:

Sing: ti ti ti ka ti   ti ti ta   ta - m ti   ti ka ti ta
Tap: ✗   ✗   ✗ ✗   ✗ ✗   ✗   ✗

2 Rhythm Singback/Clapback:

3 Rhythmic Dictation:

Write corrections above your work—don't erase!

4 Meter Identification:

a) ☐ duple   b) ☑ duple
    ☑ triple   ☐ triple

5 Editing:

Sound Advice Level 3   Ear-Training Answer Key

Ear-Training Answer Key

Lesson 5

1 Sight Singing:

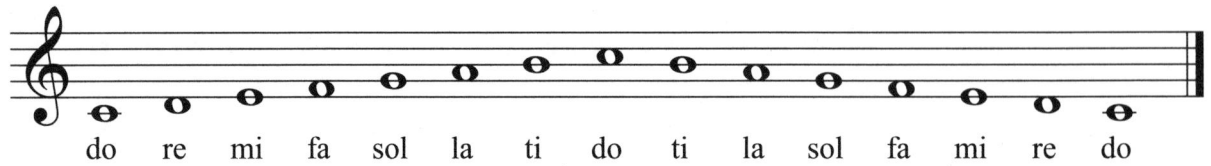

do re mi fa sol la ti do ti la sol fa mi re do

2 Sight Singing:

Sing: do — re mi re — mi fa sol fa mi re do —
Tap: x x x x x x x x x x x x

3 Editing:

4 Rhythmic Dictation:

5 Meter Identification:

a) ☑ duple
   ☐ triple

b) ☐ duple
   ☑ triple

Ear-Training Answer Key

Lesson 6

1 Sight Singing:

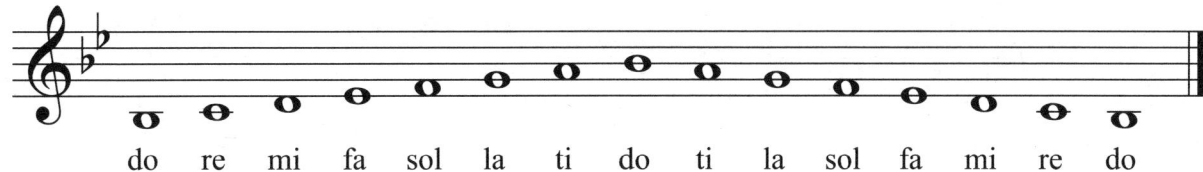

do re mi fa sol la ti do ti la sol fa mi re do

2 Sight Singing:

Sing: do re mi fa mi re mi fa sol la sol la sol fa mi re do
Tap: ✗ ✗ ✗ ✗ ✗ ✗ ✗ ✗

3 Melody Singback/Playback:

4 Rhythm Singback/Clapback:

5 Rhythmic Dictation:

6 Editing:

Ear-Training Answer Key

Lesson 7

 1 Sight Singing:

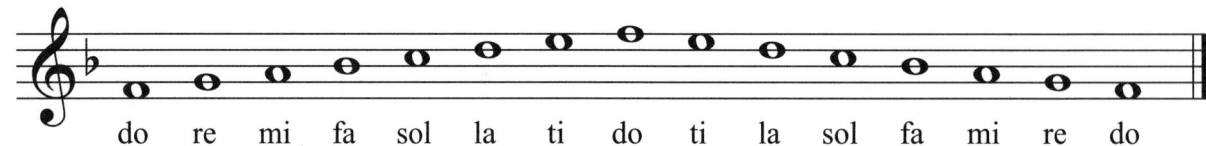

do re mi fa sol la ti do ti la sol fa mi re do

 2 Sight Singing:

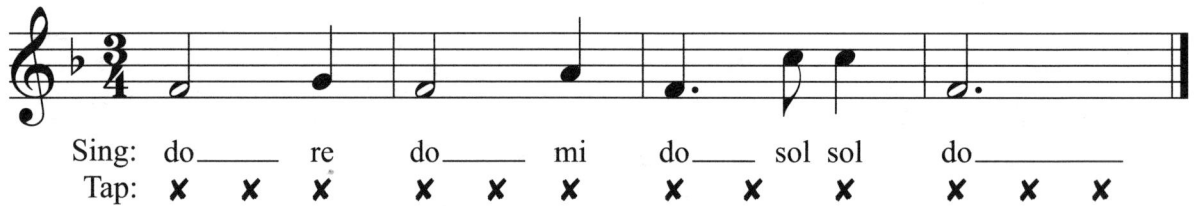

Sing: do___ re do___ mi do___ sol sol do___
Tap: ✗ ✗ ✗ ✗ ✗ ✗ ✗ ✗ ✗ ✗ ✗ ✗

 3 Interval Identification:

a) maj 3   b) P5   c) maj 2   d) maj 3   e) P5   f) maj 2   g) P5

 4 Rhythmic Clapback:

Melody:    Rhythm:

 5 Melody Singback/Playback:

Ear-Training Answer Key

Lesson 8

 1 Sight Singing:

do re mi fa sol la ti do ti la sol fa mi re do

2 Sight Singing:

Sing: sol do___ re mi re do sol sol fa mi re do ti do___
Tap: x   x   x   x   x   x   x   x   x   x   x   x   x   x

 3 Interval Identification:

a) maj 2   b) P4   c) maj 3   d) P5   e) maj 3   f) P4   g) maj 2

4 Interval Identification:

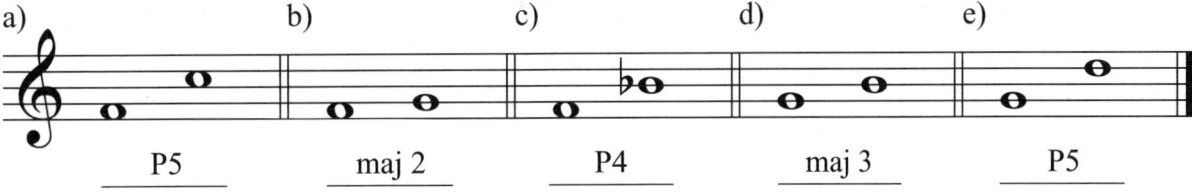

a) P5   b) maj 2   c) P4   d) maj 3   e) P5

 5 Rhythmic Dictation:

Sound Advice Level 3 — Ear-Training Answer Key — 129

Ear-Training Answer Key

Lesson 9

 1 **Sight Singing:**

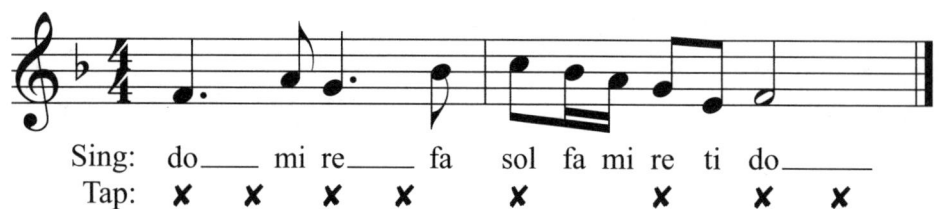

 2 **Interval Identification:**

a) maj 2   b) maj 2   c) min 2   d) maj 2   e) min 2   f) min 2   g) maj 2

 3 **Editing:**

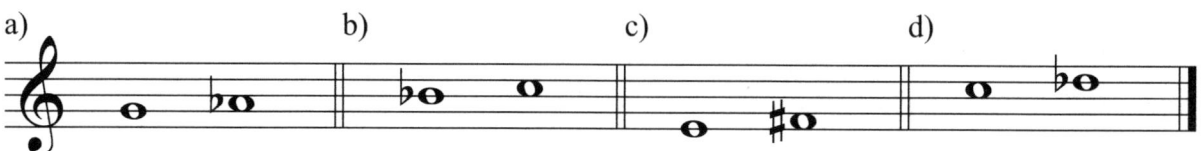

 4 **Melodic Dictation:**

 5 **Rhythmic Dictation:**

Ear-Training Answer Key

Lesson 10

 1 Interval Identification:

a) maj 2   b) P4   c) min 2   d) P5   e) maj 3   f) min 2   g) P4

 2 Sight Singing:

 3 Error Detection:

 4 Melodic Dictation:

 5 Melody Singback/Playback:

Ear-Training Answer Key

Lesson 11

 1 **Sight Singing:**

 2 **Interval Identification:**

a) maj 3   b) min 3   c) maj 2   d) min 2   e) min 3   f) min 2   g) maj 3

 3 **Editing:**

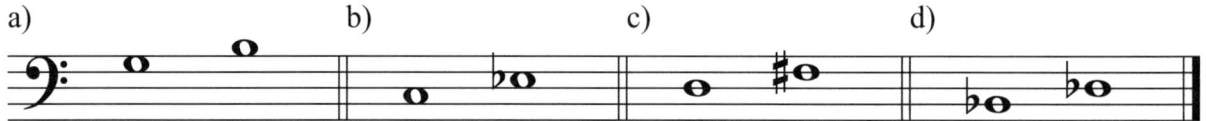

 4 **Melodic Dictation:**

 5 **Rhythmic Dictation:**

Ear-Training Answer Key

Lesson 12

 1 **Interval Identification:**

a) ↗ min 2 b) ↗ P4 c) ↗ maj 3 d) ↘ min 3 e) ↗ P5 f) ↗ maj 2 g) ↘ min 3

 2 **Sight Singing:**

 3 **Triads:**

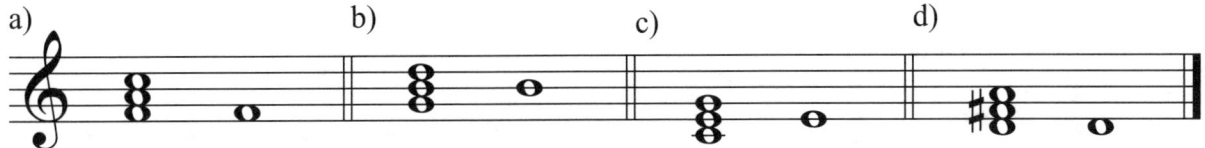

 4 **Error Detection:**

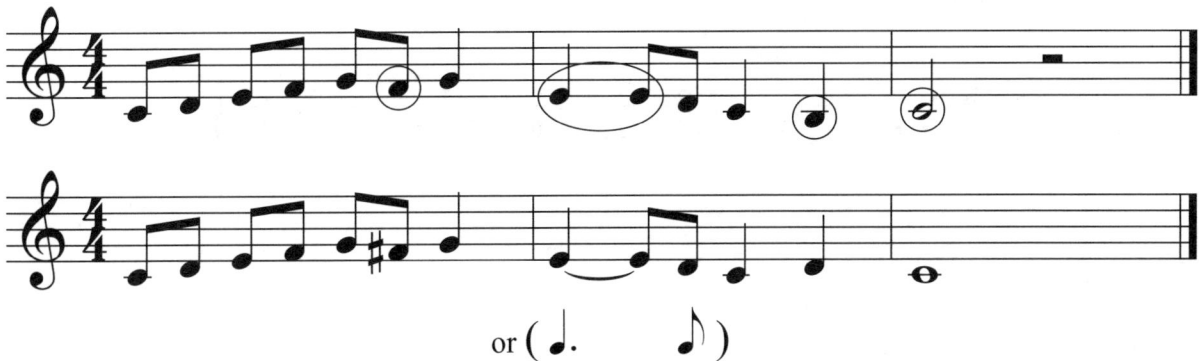

 5 **Editing:**

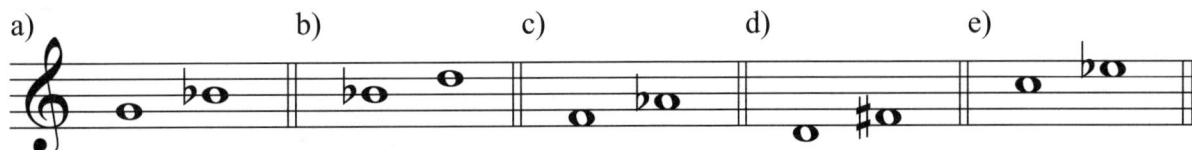

Ear-Training Answer Key

Lesson 13

 1 **Interval Identification:**

a) ↗ maj 3   b) ↘ P4   c) ↗ min 2   d) ↘ maj 2   e) ↗ P4

f) ↘ min 3   g) ↗ P5   h) ↗ maj 3   i) ↘ P4   j) ↘ maj 2

 2 **Sight Singing:**

 3 **Rhythmic Dictation:**

Melody: Rhythm:

 4 **Melodic Dictation:**

 **5** **Melody Improvisation:**

There are many other possible responses.

Ear-Training Answer Key

Lesson 14

1 **Interval Identification:**

    a) ↗ P5   b) ↘ maj 2   c) ↗ P4   d) ↘ min 3   e) ↗ maj 3

    f) ↘ P4   g) ↗ maj 2   h) ↘ P5   i) ↗ min 2   j) ↘ P5

2 **Triad Identification:**

    a) maj   b) maj   c) min   d) maj   e) min

3 **Sight Singing:**

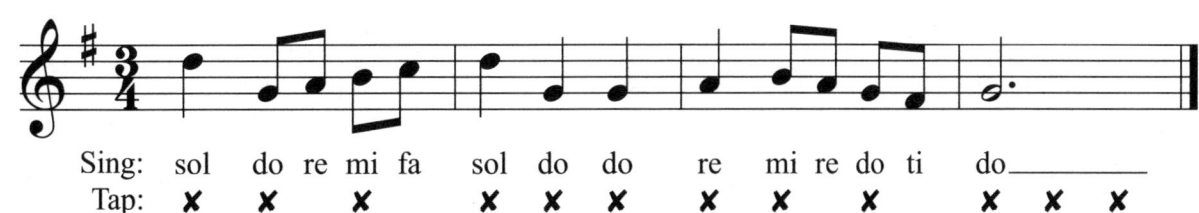

4 **Rhythmic Dictation:**

5 **Error Detection:**

Sound Advice Level 3   Ear-Training Answer Key   135

Ear-Training Answer Key

Lesson 15

1 **Interval Identification:**

a) ↘ P4   b) ↘ maj 2   c) ↗ min 3   d) ↗ P4   e) ↘ min 3

f) ↘ P5   g) ↗ maj 2   h) ↗ P5   i) ↘ maj 2   j) ↘ P5

2 **Triad Identification:**

a) min   b) maj   c) min   d) min   e) maj

3 **Triads:**

4 **Rhythmic Reading:**

Sing: ti ti ti ti   ti   ti   ti ka ti ka ti   ti ta
Tap: ✗   ✗   ✗   ✗   ✗   ✗   ✗   ✗

5 **Rhythmic Identification:**

6 **Rhythmic Dictation:**

7 **Melodic Improvisation:**

Opening: Possible response:

Ear-Training Answer Key

Lesson 16

 1 **Interval Identification:**

a) ↘ min 3   b) ↘ P8   c) ↘ maj 2   d) ↘ P5   e) ↘ P4

f) ↗ min 2   g) ↗ P5   h) ↗ maj 3   i) ↗ P8   j) ↗ maj 2

 2 **Rhythmic Reading:**

Sing: ti ti ti ka ti ka   ka ti ka ta   ka ti ka   ka ti ka ti ti ta
Tap: x x   x   x   x x   x   x

 3 **Rhythmic Dictation:**

 4 **Triad Identification:**

a) min   b) maj   c) min   d) min   e) maj

 5 **Triads:**

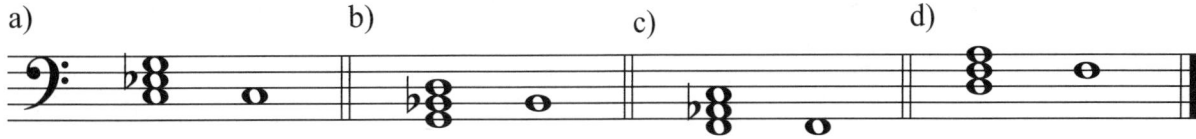

 6 **Error Detection:**

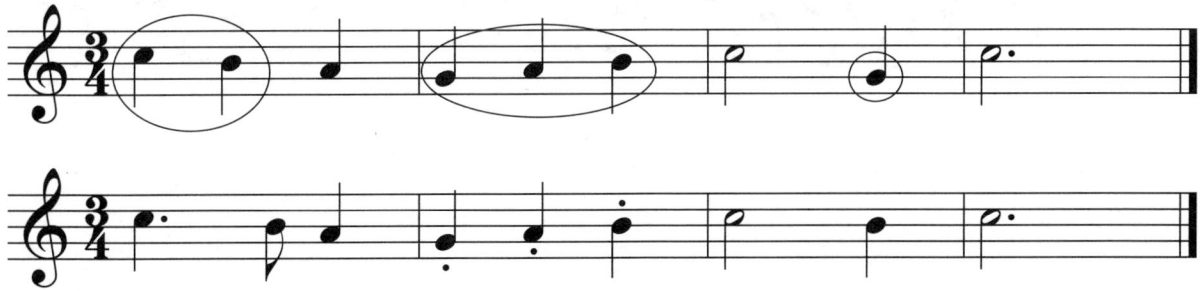

Ear-Training Answer Key

Lesson 17

1 Interval Identification:

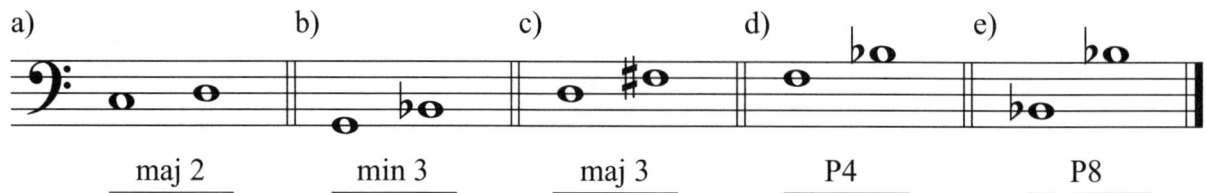

2 Rhythmic Dictation:

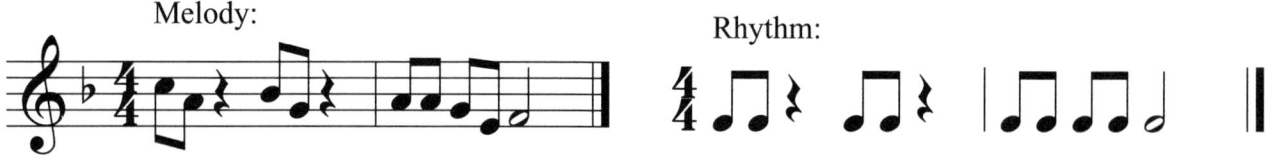

3 Melodic Dictation:

4 Rhythmic Improvisation:

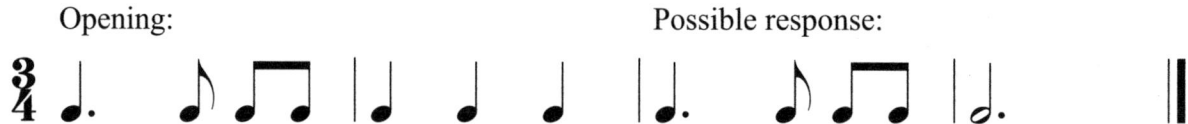

5 Melodic Improvisation:

Ear-Training Answer Key

Lesson 18

1 **Interval Identification:**

a) ↗ maj 3   b) ↗ maj 6   c) ↘ min 3   d) ↗ P8   e) ↗ maj 6

f) ↗ min 3   g) ↗ P8   h) ↘ P4   i) ↘ maj 2   j) ↗ maj 6

2 **Triads:**

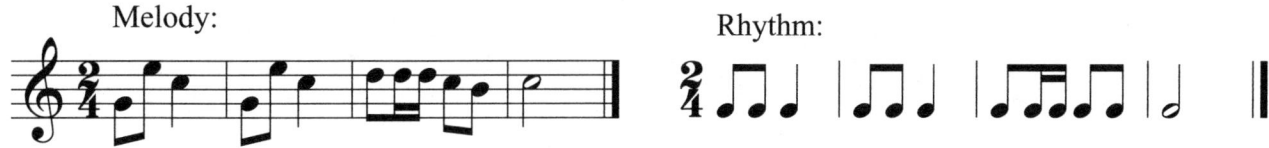

3 **Rhythmic Dictation:**

4 **Melodic Dictation:**

5 **Melodic Improvisation:**

Ear-Training Answer Key

Lesson 19

 1 **Interval Identification:**

a) ↘ maj 2   b) ↘ P4   c) ↘ min 3   d) ↘ P5   e) ↘ P8

f) ↗ maj 2   g) ↗ P4   h) ↗ maj 6   i) ↗ min 3   j) ↗ P8

 2 **Sight Singing:**

 3 **Rhythmic Dictation:**

Melody: Rhythm:

4 **Melody Singback/Playback:**

5 **Texture Identification:**

a) ☑ polyphonic   b) ☐ polyphonic
   ☐ homophonic   ☑ homophonic

Ear-Training Answer Key

Lesson 20

1. Interval Identification:

a) ↗ maj 3   b) ↗ maj 7   c) ↗ P4   d) ↗ min 2   e) ↗ maj 6

f) ↘ P5   g) ↘ maj 2   h) ↘ P8   i) ↘ min 3   j) ↘ P4

2. Sight Singing:

3. Rhythmic Dictation:

Melody:

Rhythm:

4. Melody Singback/Playback:

5. Texture Identification:

a) ☐ polyphonic   b) ☑ polyphonic
   ☑ homophonic   ☐ homophonic

Ear-Training Answer Key

Lesson 21

1 Interval Identification:

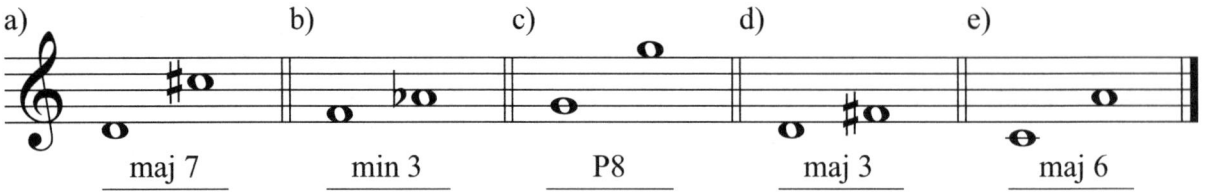

a) maj 7   b) min 3   c) P8   d) maj 3   e) maj 6

2 Melodic Improvisation:

Opening: Possible response:

3 Rhythmic Dictation:

4 Error Detection:

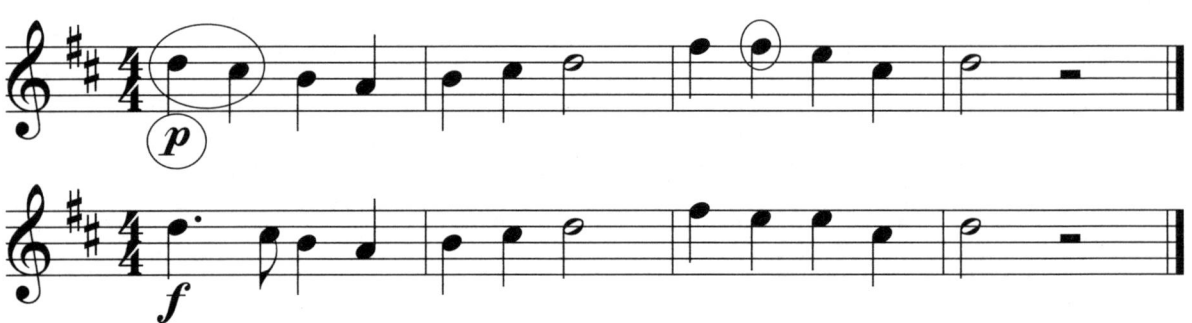

5 Texture Identification:

a) ☑ polyphonic   b) ☐ polyphonic
   ☐ homophonic   ☑ homophonic

Ear-Training Answer Key

Lesson 22

1 Interval Identification:

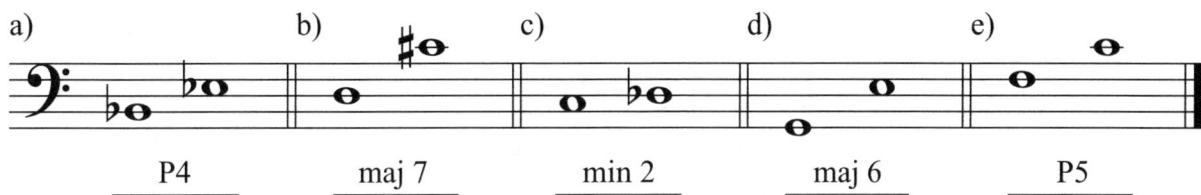

P4   maj 7   min 2   maj 6   P5

2 Melodic Improvisation:

Opening: Possible response:

3 Rhythmic Dictation:

4 Error Detection:

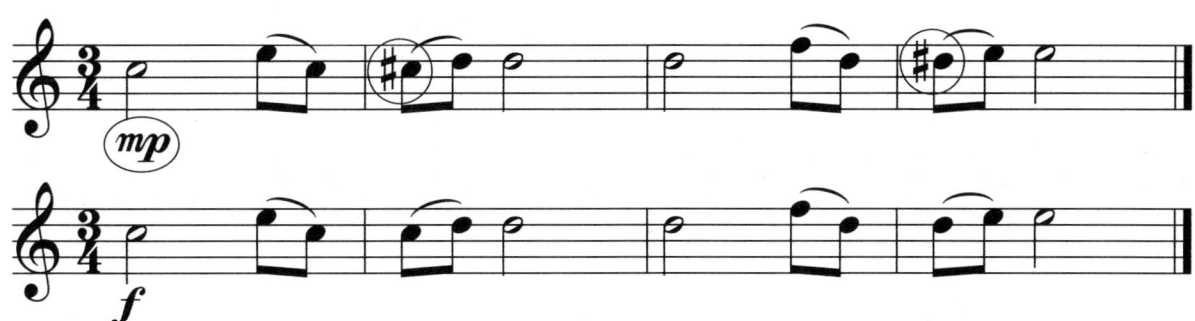

5 Texture Identification:

a) ☑ polyphonic   b) ☐ polyphonic
    ☐ homophonic   ☑ homophonic

Sound Advice Level 3   Ear-Training Answer Key   143

Ear-Training Answer Key

Lesson 23

1 **Interval Identification:**

    a) ↘ min 3   b) ↘ P8   c) ↗ maj 2   d) ↗ maj 6   e) ↗ P8

    f) ↘ P5   g) ↘ maj 2   h) ↗ maj 3   i) ↗ maj 7   j) ↗ P4

2 **Sight Singing:**

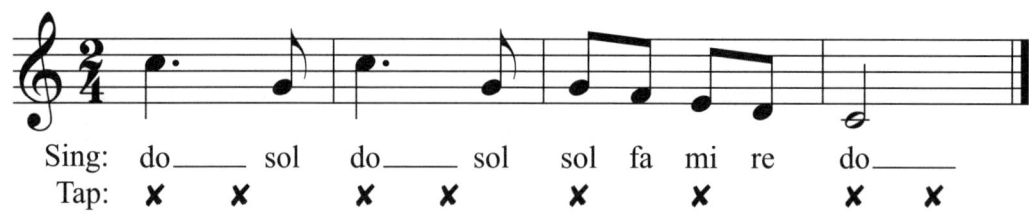

3 **Melodic Dictation:**

4 **Triads:**

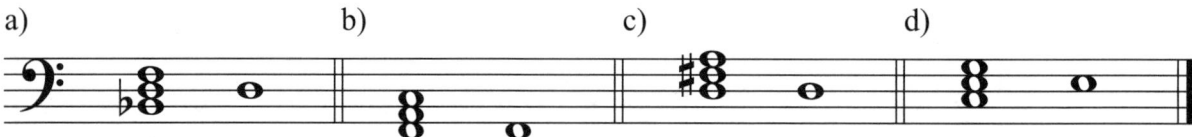

5 **Texture Identification:**

    a) ☐ polyphonic   b) ☑ polyphonic
       ☑ homophonic   ☐ homophonic

Ear-Training Answer Key

Lesson 24

1 **Interval Identification:**

    a) ↗ min 2   b) ↗ maj 6   c) ↗ maj 2   d) ↘ min 3   e) ↗ maj 3

    f) ↗ P5   g) ↗ P4   h) ↘ P4   i) ↘ maj 2   j) ↗ maj 7

2 **Triads:**

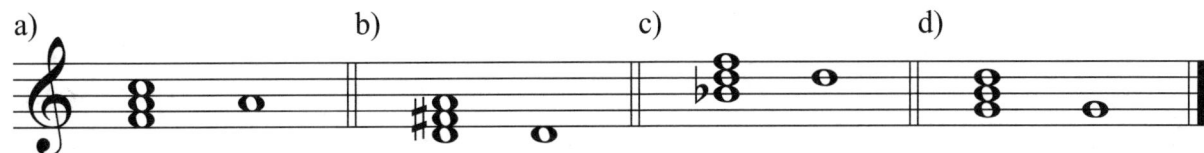

3 **Rhythmic Dictation:**

4 **Melodic Dictation:**

5 **Error Detection:**

Melody Master Answer Key

Set One

a) The following melody is in C major, in $\frac{4}{4}$ time.

b) The following melody is in F major, in $\frac{3}{4}$ time.

c) The following melody is in G major, in $\frac{2}{4}$ time.

d) The following melody is in D major, in $\frac{4}{4}$ time.

e) The following melody is in B♭ major, in $\frac{3}{4}$ time.

Check the appropriate box on p. 110.

Set Two

a) The following melody is in C major, in $\frac{3}{4}$ time.

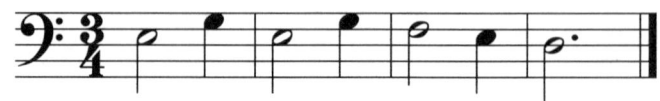

b) The following melody is in D major, in $\frac{3}{4}$ time.

c) The following melody is in F major, in $\frac{4}{4}$ time.

d) The following melody is in G major, in $\frac{3}{4}$ time.

e) The following melody is in B♭ major, in $\frac{4}{4}$ time.

Check the appropriate box on p. 110.

Melody Master Answer Key

Set Three

a) The following melody is in C major, in 3/4 time.

b) The following melody is in F major, in 4/4 time.

c) The following melody is in G major, in 4/4 time.

d) The following melody is in B♭ major, in 3/4 time.

e) The following melody is in C major, in 4/4 time.

Check the appropriate box on p. 110.

Set Four

a) The following melody is in C major, in 2/4 time.

b) The following melody is in B♭ major, in 2/4 time.

c) The following melody is in F major, in 2/4 time.

d) The following melody is in G major, in 2/4 time.

e) The following melody is in D major, in 2/4 time.

Check the appropriate box on p. 110.

Melody Master Answer Key

Set Five

 a) The following melody is in G major, in 4/4 time.

 b) The following melody is in F major, in 2/4 time.

 c) The following melody is in C major, in 3/4 time.

 d) The following melody is in D major, in 3/4 time.

 e) The following melody is in B♭ major, in 4/4 time.

Check the appropriate box on p. 110.

Mad Music Answer Key

Mad Music Chart

Name the 2nds (major or minor).

Sound Advice Level 3

Appendix

Sight-Singing Syllable Systems

Movable Do

In the *movable do* system, do represents the tonic or first degree of the scale, regardless of key. Accidentals are accounted for by changing the syllables.

The syllables for the movable do system are:

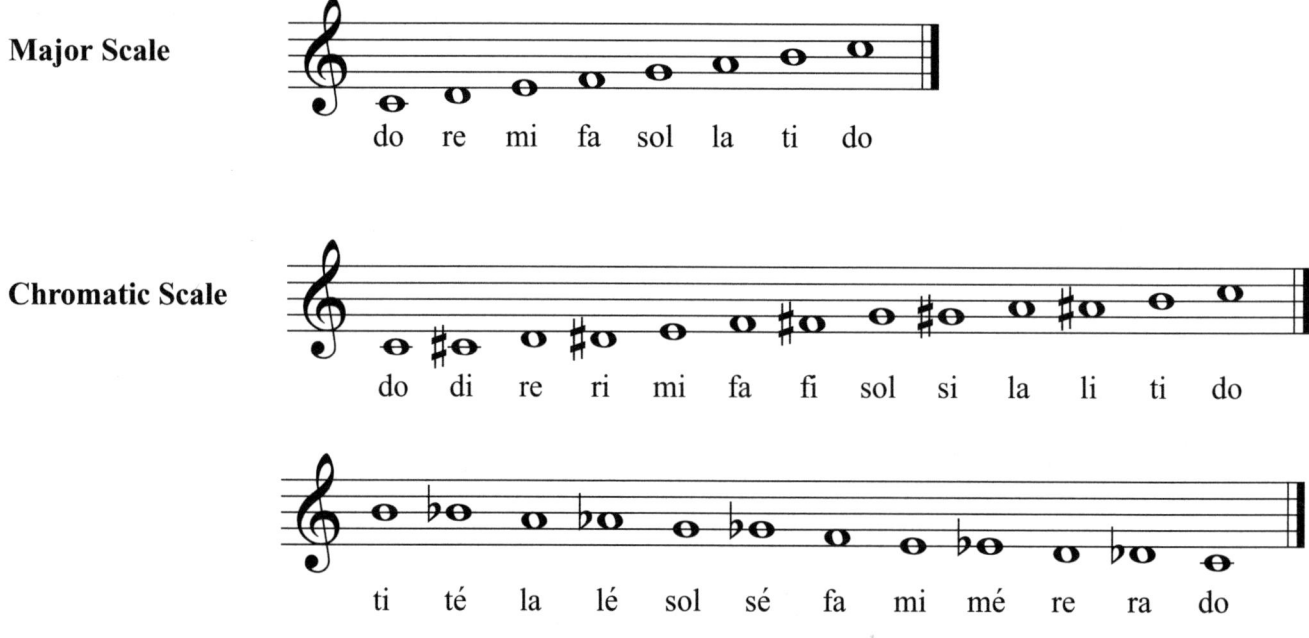

Numbers

In this system, numbers ($\hat{1}$, $\hat{2}$, $\hat{3}$, etc.) are used instead of syllables (do, re, mi, etc.). A carat (^) above a number identifies that number as a scale degree. The tonic or first degree of the scale is always $\hat{1}$, regardless of key. There is no numerical change for chromatic notes on the same degree of the scale.

Fixed Do

In the *fixed do* system, the syllables coincide with letter names of the notes, regardless of key. For example, C is always do, F is always fa, and so on. The syllables used in the fixed do system are the same as those shown above for the chromatic scale.